D1037294

The Day of
the Peacock

The Day of the Peacock

Style for Men 1963-1973

GEOFFREY AQUILINA ROSS

V&A PUBLISHING

First published by V&A Publishing, 2011
V&A Publishing
Victoria and Albert Museum
South Kensington
London SW7 2RL

Hardback edition
ISBN 978 1 85177 600 9

Library of Congress Control Number 2009932298

10 9 8 7 6 5 4 3 2 1
2014 2013 2012 2011

A catalogue record for this book is available from the British Library.

Designed by Society

V&A Photography by V&A Photographic Studio

Printed in China

V&A Publishing
Victoria and Albert Museum
South Kensington
London SW7 2RL
www.vandabooks.com

Cover Corin Redgrave, actor, soon after appearing as Lord Cardigan's aide-de-camp in Tony Richardson's 1968 film *The Charge of the Light Brigade*, wearing double-breasted, knee-length coney coat with mink collar, 80gns at Cue, Austin Reed, Regent Street. Thirties patterned silk scarf, £6 15s, at Mr Fish, Clifford Street, and beige velours trilby, 6gns, at Herbert Johnson, Bond Street. Photograph: Peter Rand.

Title page Multi-coloured striped Lurex shirt with matching tie, £15 15s and £3 3s at Mr Fish, Clifford Street. *Men in Vogue*, Autumn/Winter 1969.

Page 6 Barry Fantoni caricature of Geoffrey Aquilina Ross, *Swinging London: A Guide to Where the Action is*, London 1967.

Quotes in the text without citation are taken from interviews with the author made between May and August 2009.

Contents

Acknowledgements

Geoffrey Aquilina Ross

This book would not have been possible without the collective memories of those of us living and working in London as the Peacock Revolution took place. None of us knew at the time that the movement towards social change and a general interest in men's fashion were to be as defining as they proved to be, nor the lasting effect they would have on the future of the menswear industry and the retail business. For us the changes were a matter of fact, not importance.

This was a period driven by amateurs with a talent for catching the flamboyant moment with a mixture of energy and fun. The plethora of designer labels that go into the makings of the fashion industry today do so with a commercial reality that was little understood at this defining moment in fashion history.

I would like to thank the following for adding their recollections to mine; we were there. Sadly photographs, magazines, catalogues and mementos at the time seemed to have little historical importance or relevance to us, so little remains. Few knew then that we were meant to keep records.

If some of the facts recalled in the book contain errors, these are entirely due my flawed recollection of the period. I am indebted to those who have helped to bring the years back to life: Mary Bee, Audie Charles, Felicity Clark, Anthony Crickmay, Erica Crome, George Debono, Billy Edwards, Trisha Edwards, Barry Fantoni, Leslie Fish, Philip Fish, Bill Franks, Tom Gilbey, Peter Golding, Felicity Green, David Harvey, Min Hogg, Barbara Hulanicki, Robert Jennings, Rupert Lycett Green, Angus McGill, Chrissie Messenger, Austin Mutti Mewse, Eric Musgrave with his incomparable library of pertinent books, Rudi Patterson, John Pearse, Gawain Rainey, Jane Rainey, Michael Rainey, Ray Rathbone, Cikki Robertson, Barrie Scott, Alasdair Scott Sutherland, Ken Thomson, the Turnbull & Asser Archive, Barney Wan, Tim Wapshott, Nigel Waymouth, Kenneth Williams, Martin Wise, Colin Woodhead and Antoine Xuereb. If I have omitted a name, I apologise. The memory plays tricks.

September 2010

Foreword

Christopher Breward
Head of Research at the V&A

Geoffrey Aquilina Ross's first-hand account of the extraordinary renaissance in men's fashion that occurred in 1960s London is a timely addition to the literature on British dandyism. It complements both the trio of 'insider-authored' books that captured the sartorial spirit of the times as they were happening (Hardy Amies' *ABC of Men's Fashion*, Rodney Bennett-England's *Dress Optional* and Nik Cohn's *Today There Are No Gentlemen*)[1] and a more recent re-visiting of the traditions of postwar and contemporary menswear by fashion writers including Alice Cicolini, Hywel Davies and James Sherwood.[2] A broader engagement with the development of male dress and beauty by social and cultural historians, philosophers, art historians and sociologists has emerged in the past decade, giving rise to a sense that the 'specialist' interest that defined the field fifty years ago has finally filtered into the mainstream.[3] Who now could consider the pressing issue of fashion as a social, economic and design phenomenon without paying due attention to men as producers, critics and consumers of clothes and related commodities?

Aquilina Ross is in a better position than many to explain the ways in which the guilty secrets of the male wardrobe were eventually transformed into pleasures that all men could enjoy without fear of censure or ridicule. As the first men's fashion editor of British *Vogue* and merchandise editor of its glamorous, but sadly short-lived, companion *Men in Vogue*, he was at the epicentre of the momentous changes affecting fashion culture in the mid-1960s. Besides contributing to *Vogue* in its heyday, Aquilina Ross also provided an editorial steer for Michael Heseltine's pioneering lifestyle magazine *Town* and was the first weekly columnist on issues sartorial for the *Evening Standard*. He was a visiting lecturer at the Royal College of Art at the moment when Janey Ironside introduced men's fashion onto the curriculum and went on to lead the innovative fashion journalism course at what was then Saint Martin's School of Art. Through all of this Aquilina Ross was a colleague and friend to most of the great names in the men's fashion scene in London (not to mention those in Europe and the United States) and this is what makes his original reflections on the times so valuable. They are, in effect, a personal memoir of a turning point in the history of British fashion that still directs attitudes to fashionable masculinity in the twenty-first century.

But it is also necessary to consider how Aquilina Ross's *Day of the Peacock* fits into a longer story of British dandyism and masculine vanity, the material evidence for which survives in the V&A's collection of male clothing. The Peacock's predecessors left a legacy of striking sartorial innovations dating from the seventeenth century on, and many of these find conscious or accidental echoes in the cut, pattern and detail of 1960s dress. The rakes and fops of the 1690s, together with the notorious Macaronis (the satirical name attached to British men of fashion who adopted continental modes of dressing and behaving) of the

Opposite Blades' suit in cream. London, 1968 (V&A: T.702, A&B-1974).

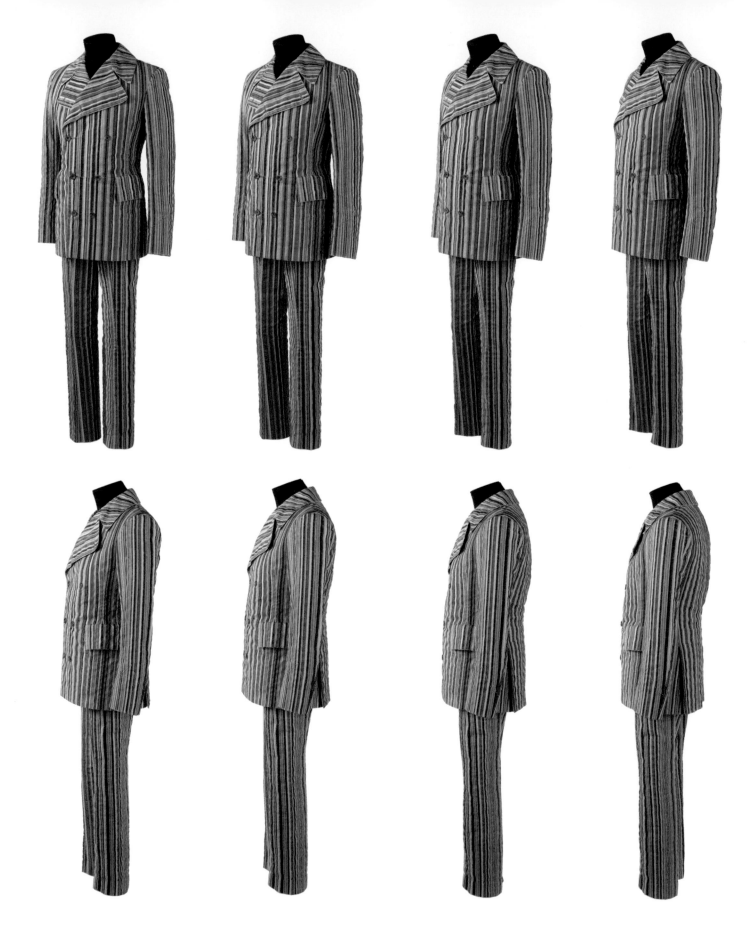

1760s and 70s, all adopted extravagant forms of self-presentation that were echoed in the streets of Mayfair and St James's over 200 years later. The needle lace shirt frills, ruffles and cuffs that decorated the necks and wrists of young gallants in the eighteenth century were revived as accompaniments to the opulent suits produced by Rupert Lycett Green of Blades (p.8) and Michael Fish (p.10) in the late 1960s. And one can see in the figured silk and printed corduroy of both these pieces references to the fine French and Spitalfields textiles chosen for formal wear by Hanoverian courtiers. Similarly the Indian, Afghan and other 'exotic' fabrics that were so influential in the dressing habits of hippies and bohemians in Swinging London find their antecedents in the painted cotton banyans (above right) and embroidered waistcoats (for example V&A: T.217–1953) that were produced in India for the European market throughout the 1700s.

The survival of these ostentatious flourishes in the later products of London's Carnaby Street and the King's Road, captured so perfectly in the 'frilly nylon', 'polka-dots' and 'stripes' of the Kinks' 1966 pop single 'A Dedicated Follower of Fashion', can be explained both by the continuation of a very English 'aristocratic' taste that has influenced the idiosyncratic fashion choices of upper-class men without interruption over three centuries; and a more popular celebration of the bawdy and colourful eighteenth-century lifestyle promoted in films such as Tony Richardson's *Tom Jones* of 1963, an adaptation of Henry Fielding's eighteenth-

century classic.[4] Starring Albert Finney as the eponymous hero, this satirical romp was as much an affectionate critique of the new sexual and social mores of fashionable 1960s London as it was a skilful interpretation of one of the first English novels. And though set in the early nineteenth century, Lionel Bart's hugely successful musical *Oliver!*, filmed in 1968, also demonstrated a contemporary interest in and connection with the tatterdemalion glamour of historical men's dress.

Our 1960s Peacocks were not only inspired by the more extreme flourishes of eighteenth-century men's clothing, however. Those in the know also looked to the more austere registers of nineteenth-century dandyism and the imperial glories of military uniform. The mode of dressing introduced to London and the rest of Europe by Beau Brummell (1778–1840) and his followers around 1805 offered a sober but no less expensive and refined alternative to the extravagance of earlier elite masculine styles (p.12). The Brummellian morning dress of top boots and buckskin breeches, dark blue coat and buff-coloured waistcoat with bright white linens, together with the blue coat, white waistcoat and black pantaloons buttoned tight to the ankle over silk stockings that passed for evening wear, may have seemingly put an end to the first era of Peacock dressing. Paradoxically, however, this highly sophisticated switch to minimal decoration and fine tailoring, which subsequent commentators have erroneously characterized as the 'great masculine renunciation' of fashion, in fact set a

Opposite Mr Fish corduroy suit. Britain, c.1968 (V&A: T.310–1979).

Above Man's nightgown (banyan) in chintz. Coromandel Coast (tailored in the Netherlands or England), 1750–75 (V&A: T.215–1992).

template for modern sartorial beauty that survived into the 1960s when a new generation of innovative tailors and retailers were looking for inspiration. Indeed John Stephen, the 'King of Carnaby Street', made conscious reference to the knee-length double-breasted frock coat of the nineteenth-century dandy in his sleek worsted suit of 1970 (above right).

It is possible to see a similar preoccupation with the pared down elegance of Victorian and Edwardian dandyism in the cool mohair minimalism of Mod styling, or the return to favour among students and art-school types of button-down shirt collars, short boxy tweed jackets and narrow white trousers (as sported by the Rolling Stones in John French's 1964 photograph of the group with model Pattie Boyd, wearing a Mary Quant dress, see p.17). But a nostalgic preference for the louder elements of the nineteenth-century dressing-up box, as embodied by striped flannel boating blazers and bandsmen's tunics (above left), generally prevailed in the wider realm of 1960s pop and fashion culture. Robert Orbach, director of the Portobello Road and Soho store I Was Lord Kitchener's Valet, recalls:

[We sold] second-hand fur coats, pith helmets ... general junk, some good and some bad. Some people liked wearing second-hand clothes but at first it wasn't that busy. Then over a period of time, clothes started to take over from the furniture. Eric Clapton was the first one to buy a military jacket early in 1966 ... And Mick

Jagger bought a red Grenadier guardsman drummer's jacket ... They all came from Moss Bros and British Army Surplus. In 1966 it was only fifty or so years from ... when we had an Empire ... So Mick bought this tunic and wore it on Ready, Steady, Go! ... *performing* Paint it Black. *The next morning there was a line of about 100 people wanting to buy the tunic ... and we sold everything in the shop by lunchtime.*[5]

In some ways one could argue that the period Aquilina Ross describes was the final flowering of old-style dandyism, a moment when the dandy stance shifted from a closed and aristocratic to a more democratic context, when dandyism simply came to mean the donning of fancy-dress ruffles and retro-chic militaria by anyone who could afford boutique prices. Accessible and witty journalism, alongside the creativity of designers and shop-owners, allowed this opening up to happen and this book is a marvellous 'insider guide' to the key developments and personalities involved.

Notes

1 Hardy Amies, *ABC of Men's Fashion* (London, 1964), Rodney Bennett-England, *Dress Optional: A Revolution in Menswear* (London, 1967), Nik Cohn, *Today There Are No Gentlemen: The Changes in Englishmen's Clothes since the War* (London, 1971).
2 Alice Cicolini, *The New English Dandy* (London, 2005), Hywel Davies, *Modern Menswear* (London, 2008), James Sherwood, *The London Cut: Savile Row Bespoke Tailoring* (Venice, 2007).
3 Peter McNeil and Vicki Karaminas (eds), *The Men's Fashion Reader* (Oxford, 2009).
4 *The Story of Tom Jones, a Foundling*, 1749.
5 See further at <vam.ac.uk/collections/fashion/features/1960s/interviews/orbach_interview>

Opposite **Double-breasted dress coat. Britain, 1810–20 (V&A: T.738, A&B-1913).**
Above **Boating suit. Britain, 1890–1900 (V&A: T.113, A&B-1934).**

Above **John Stephen suit and jacket. Britain, 1970 (V&A: T.214:1–4–1997).**

Changing Times

It was early in the 1960s – the decade that would be hailed as the Swinging Sixties – when journalists and social commentators became aware of flamboyant changes taking place in the way many middle-class men in London dressed. As if overnight it was as acceptable for men to take care about how they dressed as it was for women. Even men with what might seem to be impeachable social (and heterosexual) backgrounds were going about their daily lives wearing velvet suits, or jackets, accessorized with brightly coloured, flowing silk scarves. Their hair was longer, too. Until then, all men had been conventional, comfortably wearing the clothes expected of their professions, and visiting their barbers for a precision trim in a fortnightly routine. You could invariably tell a man's occupation by the way he dressed.

But now London revitalized itself; its focus changed. Youth was the key and young people with ideas and ambition were forging ahead, appearing to challenge all that had gone before. From many young men there seemed to be a growing demand for a more liberated choice of clothes that would match the radical change in women's fashion, with its new-found freedom and exuberance, fired by young designers like Mary Quant. Quant had triumphantly challenged traditional strongholds when she opened her first Bazaar boutique in Chelsea's King's Road in 1955. Her clothes were nothing like those worn by her customers' mothers. They were young, colourful, sexy and often expensive, made from fabrics not normally worn by middle-class women.

This male revolution, if that is what it was, was led by a similar liberator, John Stephen, who opened his first Carnaby Street shop catering for fashionable middle-class males in 1956, a year after Quant's first intrepid steps. Stephen was to be the catalyst for men's fashion. Until his arrival, even if men had wanted colourful clothes, there was little available that was ready-made; stagnation in men's style was due to lack of opportunity. Generally young British men wore what their fathers wore. With few exceptions they looked, dressed and, in all likelihood, behaved, as their fathers did. Conformity was the key. If their fathers' clothes had changed little in style or colour over the decades, why would theirs?

But however stylishly Stephen's customers may have dressed, offering a small group of shops a steady income, they were not influential outside their own confines – unlike the emerging flamboyant breed of socially well-connected young men that was predominantly upper-class and visible daily on the smarter streets of London. In what was a natural progression, these were the men who took the concept of fashion for men one step further, to legitimacy. Attempting to attach a label to this swaggering moment of innovation, media commentators settled on the term 'Peacock Revolution'. The Day of the Peacock had arrived.

In her book *The Peacock's Tail* published in 1958, Pearl Binder examined the purpose and meaning of male dress since primitive times and lamented the passing of the days when Savile Row tailors influenced well-dressed men but, ending the book with a note of optimism, she said she believed Britain was ready for a Peacock revival (capital 'P'). She was right, although the outcome was possibly not quite as she had imagined. The colourful explosion that characterized the 1960s did have a ripple effect on well-mannered Savile Row, but little more than that until Peacock tailors set up shop there, too. However, this foppish outburst caused an extraordinary rebirth of fashion that was to have a lasting social and commercial effect, and was the begetter, the progenitor, of the remarkable selection of clothes and designer shops available to men today. It was this upper-class fashion movement that gave manufacturers and store buyers a confident new lease of life and gave designers the loose reins they needed.

Before this Peacock resurgence, any changes in the way a fashionable man dressed evolved slowly. Classic formality and conventional turn-out was regarded as the sign of being well dressed, of being a gentleman. Fashion was not a word much used in the context of men's clothes. Until this point, whatever his age, any changes to a man's wardrobe were suggested by dedicated tailors, shirt-makers and haberdashers, who understood style and tradition. In upper-class society the accepted rule was dark suits for town or city, brown suits and tweeds for the country. In town shirts were either blue or white in colour and had stiff, starched, detachable collars. Only the bold addition of a colourful tie,

purchased at a reputable shop or department store, was permitted: this showed a sign of individuality that was much admired. In the country, clothes were to appear functional, the colder the winter, the heavier the tweed. Tattersall check shirts (the check was named after Richard Tattersall, who used the pattern for his horse blankets) were always acceptable. The only time a man might be encouraged to break these sartorial strictures would be when entertaining at home, or while on holiday, when invariably he would wear items selected by his wife, mother, sisters or girlfriend.

That was really as far as personal liberation permitted a man to go. Anything more showy was suspect unless you were an actor or artist or, in the phrase of the times, a 'bookie'. Or perhaps the Duke of Windsor, who had a passion for clothes and, being royal, could get away with what might have been considered eccentricities. He once stunned friends by wearing a country suit in London, after which he then went on to start a number of idiosyncratic fashions such as wearing a double-breasted dinner jacket with a shawl collar, Fair Isle sweaters and brown suede shoes with a dark blue suit.

Every man who could, owned a suit. If he was wealthy, he owned many. Setting a style that was internationally recognized were London's grand, long-established tailors of Savile Row and the shirt-makers of Jermyn Street, who made every shirt to measure.

These purveyors of gentlemen's essentials sold items that were considered the height of good taste, clothes that would create the instantly recognizable image of the English Gentleman.

It was an image often supposed to have originated with Beau Brummell who, at the beginning of the nineteenth century, astounded contemporary London society – he took to wearing suits. That is to say, he teamed the immaculately tailored, dark-coloured jackets, for which he had become known, with matching trousers at a time when the norm was a colourful coat (jacket) teamed with breeches of a different colour and fabric. He wore these outfits with a white cravat that often took a dozen trial knottings to achieve perfection, and it was this dandified appearance and demeanour that brought him to the attention of the Prince of Wales, thus opening the door for his own entrance into Society. It was this exquisitely crafted image that would influence the appearance of the English Gentleman thereafter, leading some to claim that since Beau Brummell paved the way, English tailors and the nobility alike have dictated men's fashion to the rest of the world. It may be so. It was certainly an image to emulate.

Bridging the gap between Savile Row and Carnaby Street were successful West End stores such as Austin Reed, Jaeger and Simpsons, which echoed the former's club-like formal way of dressing but at lesser prices, and the flourishing high street multiples, such as Montague Burton, Hepworths, John Temple

and Fifty Shilling Tailors (known later as John Collier), which offered equivalent items at even more competitive prices. It was estimated that at their peak these multiples provided three-quarters of all suits sold to British men with social or career aspirations but small incomes. Until the mid-1960s a man could have a suit custom-made at any of these places, but 'off-the-peg' suits, as ready-made clothes were then called, accounted for an ever-increasing market share of the business: these clothes were both less expensive and immediate, avoiding months of waiting for the garment to be finished.

Innovations, when they came, were few: the introduction of ready-made formal shirts with comfortable attached collars killed off shirts with detachable, crisp white collars that sawed into the neck, the collar studs that fastened the offending collar to the shirt's neckband compounding both the pain and discomfort, fore and aft.

But as Bob Dylan sang in 1963, *The Times they are a-Changin'* – and things were changing. To general approbation men were turning into Peacocks even in the streets around Savile Row and Jermyn Street. As small independent shops opened up, fashion for men fast became a legitimate area of interest and commercial reality. Traditional values were mutating. Liberal ideas were generally appreciated and embraced, albeit often subliminally. Men were beginning to enjoy shopping for clothes. Who wanted

Above New young pop groups, like women's fashion, soon epitomized the changes created by London's swinging decade. Often a group such as the Searchers was considered the ideal accessory for a fashion shoot. Photograph: John French, 1960s.

Above Model Pattie Boyd in a Mary Quant crepe dress backed by the informally dressed Rolling Stones. Photograph: John French, April 1964.

to be conventional when, if you and your peer group were in touch with the times, there was no reason to be?

The 1960s conjure up visions of a postwar baby-boom generation, driven by a mixture of liberation and rebellion, in headlong pursuit of an alternative way of life in which sexual freedom and mini-skirts were accompanied by great music, cannabis and the whiff of the day's favourite scent, patchouli. No one knew, then, that they were at the centre of a Swinging era; they didn't know they were at the centre of anything. Money was tight, salaries were low. As a *Vogue* fashion editor I earned £900 a year, a pitifully small income when Russell & Bromley's elastic-sided Chelsea boots cost nearly £5, the same price as dinner for two in a King's Road restaurant. But the desire to have a good time was infectious. Life on little money maybe, but that's just how it was.

In her book *Paris France* (1940), Gertrude Stein claimed that between 1900 and 1939 Paris was where the twentieth century was at. Had she lived longer, she would have seen the focus of the twentieth century move to London, where fashion, theatre, the arts, the media, music, people and a renewed sense of fun allied to dilettante commercial ambition replaced the Parisian sense of intellectual and artistic freedom.

According to Christopher Booker in *The Neophiliacs* (1969), a study of the revolution in English life in the 1950s and 60s, the latter decade was marked by bright people conspiring to elevate the new above the established, obsessed with change. Perhaps. Or was he being simplistic? London, like many postwar cities, had quietly evolved into a city of opportunity where talent and grit were rewarded. Pushing aside elders and betters, young talent was raring to race ahead and have a good time doing so. Social constraints and class barriers were rapidly disappearing. London had become home to the great and the groovy from all over Britain and many luminaries – actors, directors, artists, fashion designers – would go on to lasting international fame.

Pop groups from Birmingham, Manchester and Liverpool, in particular, where a revolution through music and fashion was already in motion, arrived intent on capturing the spirit of the times. Giving the music industry a new seam of gold to mine were Gerry and the Pacemakers, the Rolling Stones, the Who, the Kinks, the Animals, the Small Faces, Herman's Hermits and many more. The Beatles, too, played their part though, in the early years they were considered just another fab group. As a rule, if you liked the Stones you probably didn't like the Beatles; in the same way, if you liked Adam Faith or Dusty Springfield you probably didn't like Cliff Richard or Petula Clark.

In 1965 David Bailey, a young photographer predestined for fame, launched his photographic *Box of Pin-Ups* with individual portraits of the names of the day. Among the 36 icons were Mick

Above Young, good looking people visiting Chelsea's burgeoning boutiques often found themselves invited to appear in the seasonal fashion shows. Fresh faces could guarantee the show coverage in morning and evening newspapers. Here, English Boy (see p.66) models, pose. Celia Birtwell collection.

Jagger, Rudolf Nureyev, David Hockney, Terence Stamp, John Lennon and Paul McCartney and, elevated to the rank of celebrity, the Kray Twins, who ruled London's East End with intimidating force. If you own this *Box*, you have a highly collectable piece of 1960s memorabilia and fashion history. All these men, even the Krays, took great care choosing their clothes. Their appeal to Bailey and to Francis Wyndham, who wrote the text, was the stylish way in which they chose to dress. Each man was a peacock in his own world.

Historically, these were tumultuous times. The 1960s have been defined as the decade of assassinations that shocked the Western world: John F. Kennedy on 22 November 1963, Martin Luther King on 4 April 1968 and Robert Kennedy on 5 June 1968. It was also the decade when the Berlin Wall was erected, Che Guevara was killed in Bolivia, Yuri Gagarin became the first man in space and, five years on, Neil Armstrong fulfilled the dream of Everyman when, on 21 July 1969, he became the first man to walk on the moon.

On a different note, the decade also conjures visions of hippie communes, Indian gurus, dance crazes like the Twist, recreational drugs such as marijuana and LSD, ley lines, Twiggy, psychedelia and free love, as well as appalling eccentricities like self-trapanation. For many, however, it is fashion that gives the period from the early 1960s to the early 1970s its stamp of lasting originality, particularly the rising importance of fashion for men.

The Day of the Peacock traces the development of men's fashion during the heady years that made London in the Sixties Swing, spearheaded by a small number of designers and entrepreneurs, from John Stephen to Michael Fish. They were the catalysts who moved the goalposts of acceptable dress for men, and provided the clothes to match. Thanks to them, a lasting – and commercially successful – fashion industry was born.

The following chapters form a chronology that traces the rise and fall of these influential designers, tailors and retailers, and also chart a journey that tracks the geographical shifts in sartorial influence from Carnaby Street (territory of the newly fashion-conscious tribe that would become known as Mods), to Savile Row (realm of establishment tailoring) to Chelsea's free-wheeling King's Road, before returning to the fold, those streets around Savile Row where, traditionally, fashionable men have always dressed.

Above The *Swingeing London* edition [*sic*] *Queen* magazine, 22 June 1966. It was an irreverent view of London following *Time* magazine's earlier trumpeting homage to the Swinging city.

Overleaf, pages 20–1 In 1971 Jermyn Street shirt-makers Turnbull & Asser introduced a range of ready-made suits elegantly tailored in flannel. They also provided the street's first ranges of ready-made shirts. Worn here by Randall Lawrence. Photograph: Norman Eales. Turnbull & Asser Archive.

TOWN

For Men 3/

August 1967

STYLE BIBLES

Magazines for Peacocks

At home to

Strippers
Whale Killers
Meter maids
Top tailors
Deep drinkers
and
Johnny
Speight
on
Swingers

With today's abundance of men's magazines majoring on both clothes and grooming, it seems extraordinary that in the 1960s, when there was such an explosion of interest in men's clothes and the media was claiming that London was leading a Peacock Revolution, there were no British publications for men with fashion as a core subject. Although changes in the way men might dress had become an expanding commercial reality for both manufacturers and retailers, consumer magazines with a men's fashion platform were not yet mainstream. A number were launched; none survived. The only magazines that covered men's clothes were dull trade magazines with a limited readership whose role was to bolster manufacturing and retailing, and whose targeted readers worked in the industry as cloth merchants, manufacturers, retailers or their various suppliers.

There were two theories for this absence. The first held that not enough men would buy or read magazines; market research suggested that magazines were felt not to be manly unless devoted exclusively to political issues, cars or football. It was women who bought magazines. The second theory claimed that there was no revenue available to support the considerable production costs involved in sustaining the birth and first few years of a man's magazine. The advent of television as a national advertising medium, coupled with the arrival of Sunday colour magazine supplements spearheaded by the *Sunday Times* in 1962, supposedly ate up all the advertising revenue. As these

media pundits pointed out, the only men's magazines that might survive were top-shelf, soft porn, 'girlie mags' that were independent of mainstream advertising.

Maybe it was simply a matter of timing. As reality was to prove decades later, the right editor with a finger on the day's pulse can make a magazine succeed, especially when there is financial support from a parent company that can promote the product as well as give it the essential funding needed to survive as readership and circulation numbers build up. In the early 1960s magazine management all too often appointed as editors professionals with excellent track records in other fields but who, when faced with finding the new breed of male readership, commissioned topics they personally found interesting rather than features that targeted the potential reader's interests or way of life. The numerous men's magazines that soldier on with some success now do so because their editors are in tune with their readers.

Men's magazines are not a new idea; there have been many over the centuries. Considered to be the world's first was Germany's *Erbauliche Monaths-Unterredungen (Edifying Monthly Discussions)*. A morally uplifting publication, it made its first appearance in 1663. Five years later *Giornale de' letterati di Roma* was published and proved a great success with the literary men of Rome.

The first publication that could be said to answer current

Opposite 'The Cool Footman' and 'The Stripper' (modelled here by Sixties' wildchild Amanda Lear) were two features in *Town*. The fashion pages covered the cream of Savile Row tailors and the new young pretenders that were their competition. *Town*, August 1967. Photograph: Clive Arrowsmith.

Above Jocelyn Stevens, in floral tie from Carnaby Street, the proprietor of Society magazine *Queen*, which reported each month on the way of life of London's smart set as well as men's fashion. *Men in Vogue*, November 1965. Photograph: Ron Traeger.

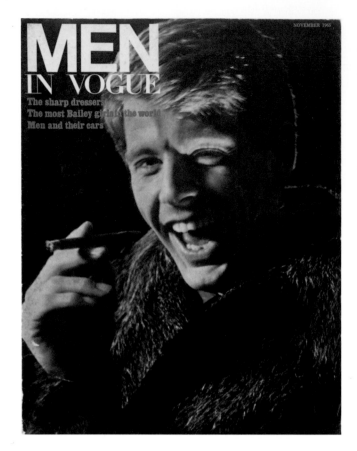

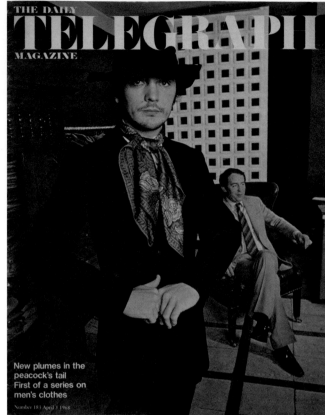

demands seems to have been England's *The Gentleman's Magazine*, which first appeared in 1731. Unlike the German and Italian publications, which were regarded as socially improving, this magazine aimed to entertain readers with essays, short stories and political comment. For anyone who collects curious facts, it is worth noticing that in Samuel Johnson's *Dictionary* of 1755, he records that it was Edward Cave, publisher of *The Gentleman's Magazine*, who first used the word 'magazine' to mean a published journal. Until then the use was strictly military: a magazine was a store for arms, ammunition and explosives.

The Victorians, as if to prove they had a wide breadth of interests, had established a kindred group of journals for men, each one making a point of providing editorial coverage of men's fashion. There was the *Gentleman's Magazine of Fashion*, for example, a well-regarded publication, as well as others with titles such as *Fancy Clothes*, the *Gentleman's Pictorial*, *The Gentleman (A Cosmopolitan Journal)*, the *County Gentleman* and *The Gentleman's Journal*. The emphasis of each one centred on the importance of being a Gentleman. Clothes, therefore, mattered. *The Gentleman's Magazine* lasted almost 200 years until the outbreak of the First World War in 1914 when it was forced to cease publication.

A revival of the genre came about in New York when *Apparel Arts* was launched in 1931. It was conceived as a quarterly for the clothing trade in general and menswear retailers in particular,

with the aim of providing information that would help them sell their merchandise. The premise was that by giving retailers visual references and product updates, their salesmen would be better able to propel prospective customers towards new clothing. However, while the magazine achieved its aim, its presentation proved so attractive that customers frequently pocketed copies to take home. On discovering this, the publishers realized that a consumer magazine for men with pages devoted to fashion could be a success on the bookstands. And so *Esquire* was born.

The first issue appeared in October 1933 and while initially it was considered racy, this editorial slant would change as the magazine turned to subjects it considered men wanted: fashion recommendations and intellectual or diverting features written by contributors such as Ernest Hemingway and F. Scott Fitzgerald. From October 1940, when the United States entered the Second World War, glamorous pin-up illustrations by Peruvian-born Alberto Vargas (who signed himself 'Varga') were added to cheer members of the armed services, especially those serving overseas. These delightful, leggy, scantily but decorously clad figures provided readers with the distraction they needed and the considerable leap in magazine sales and circulation figures that followed proved a clear indication that pin-ups could help the sales of a consumer magazine. That year the Varga calendar sold 320,000 copies. Three years later it sold one million, collectors' items every one. It was Varga's

Above To launch the first issue of *Men in Vogue* in November 1965, actor Edward Fox wore an unplucked nutria fur coat, 915gns, from Woollands, Knightsbridge. Photograph: Norman Parkinson.

Above Terence Stamp in tight black barathea suit, made-to-measure, 70gns, at Doug Hayward. Its double-breasted jacket has wide lapels edged with braiding. Hayward is seated in the background. *Daily Telegraph Magazine,* 5 April 1968. Photograph: Hans Feurer.

pin-ups that inspired the beauties painted on the fuselages of American warplanes.

Meanwhile *Apparel Arts* continued to be published to much the same formula until 1957 when, from a journal aimed exclusively at the trade, it was transformed into a quarterly consumer publication. Two years later it was renamed *Gentlemen's Quarterly* and appeared as a supplement to *Esquire*. For decades it retained its effective concentration on men's fashion and style. With its title simplified to *GQ* (earning itself the sobriquet among gay men of Giddy Queen), it became a successful American monthly. Then in 1983 it changed hands. It was sold to Condé Nast, publishers of *Vogue*, who could see the financial advantages of publishing a magazine for men but wanted to start with a solid readership base already in position. Editorial changes were immediately put in hand to alter the formula that had given it its gay nickname. Then attractive photographs of women were introduced and women given appropriate editorial coverage as well as featuring in fashion pictures alongside men, particularly on swimwear spreads. To counterbalance the clothes, manly topics that went beyond fashion were introduced. *Apparel Arts* had come a long way. Now, as *GQ*, it was in direct competition with its former sibling, *Esquire*.

A parallel though less successful resurgence in magazines containing men's fashion also occurred in Britain, possibly inspired by *Esquire*'s upward trajectory with *Apparel Arts*. (An attempt was made to establish a British edition of *Esquire* in 1953 but it folded after six years. It was successfully relaunched in 1991.)

Tailor & Cutter was, as its name implies, a clothing trade journal. Established early in the twentieth century, it had a steady, though dwindling, readership of manufacturers and retailers in the men's clothing industry. Under its ebullient editor John Taylor, the publishers launched an additional quarterly in 1952. Taylor's intention was to cover fashion as well as lifestyle for the man-about-town ('lifestyle' was a new word then), hence its title. *Man About Town* was modestly successful but in 1960 it changed hands and was snapped up by Cornmarket Press, whose proprietors Clive Labovitch and Michael Heseltine (soon to enter parliament as Conservative MP for Tavistock) hoped to build on the magazine's current, if modest, readership and establish a quality version of an archetypal men's magazine.

From these unprepossessing beginnings an impressive magazine was created. Talented young writers provided interesting features and a creative layout was designed by one of London's most adventurous art directors, Tom Wolsey, to give it visual impact. But good looking, humorous and avant-garde as it may have been, it failed to prove itself financially self-sufficient, even after a variety of editors had been called in to stamp it with their own personalities. *Man About Town* may have been highly regarded in

Above Patrick Procktor, artist, always appeared in dashing wide-brimmed hats with tailored suits. In Bond Street hatters Herbert Johnson, his choice was red velvet. *Daily Telegraph Magazine*, 5 April 1968. Photograph: Hans Feurer.

Above In the cutting rooms at Mr Fish, director Barry Sainsbury with Christopher Lynch, stylist. Sainsbury's embroidered brocade evening jacket was 65 gns to order. Slim and double-breasted, with low buttons and wide lapels, it was worn with a rollneck evening shirt. *Daily Telegraph Magazine*, 5 April 1968. Photograph: Hans Feurer.

publishing circles as a quality magazine, and certainly its content was intelligent, but it failed nonetheless to attract either sufficient circulation numbers or sufficient advertising revenue. With each relaunch, intended to revitalize its image, the editor changed, as did its title. First to *About Town*, then to *Town*. The ambition may have been to create the quintessential magazine for men, but men were not convinced. It closed in 1968.

In an interview years later Heseltine's tone was ungenerous and derogatory as he talked about his magazine:

We bought a spin-off consumer magazine from the trade title, Tailor & Cutter. *It was called* Man About Town *and had little to commend itself. It was a magazine supplement to* Tailor & Cutter. *We recruited a team to turn this tatty quarterly into a glossy monthly for men. In one sense we were ahead of the time. Men's fashion was at the margin of acceptability and men's magazines of the time relied almost entirely upon their willingness to peddle soft porn. We were not in that business. The magazine relied for revenue on the advertising industry, and on the wish of art directors and copywriters to see their work displayed in this pace-setting publication.*

The editors on *Man About Town/About Town/Town* included big names of the day: Clive Labovitch, David Hughes, Nicholas Tomalin and MP Julian Critchley, who took over the editorship when he lost his parliamentary seat and proceeded to oversee its demise in 1968.

As *Town* had proclaimed, men's fashion was now a bona fide subject. So, as Peacocks began appearing in great numbers in London's social circles, Condé Nast launched *Men in Vogue* in 1965 as an add-on quarterly supplement to British *Vogue* in order to test the market. This was done in spite of reservations on the part of the elderly management, which was firmly of the opinion that there was negligible advertising revenue to be found in a men's magazine and the venture would prove a waste of valuable resources. To ward off any misconceptions, as fashion was to be at its core, the management insisted that all accompanying editorial features be perceived as masculine – that is, heterosexual – so they appointed *Vogue*'s illustrious editor Beatrix Miller and *House & Garden*'s odd-ball editor Robert Harling as joint editors. I took on the role of *Vogue*'s first men's fashion editor. The fledgling magazine was well received but the management was vindicated. The advertising team was fully focused on the parent fashion title and so had little time to sell its new add-on quarterly; revenue was insufficient and within two years *Men in Vogue* was gone, although a column with the same name continued to appear in British *Vogue*.

Other women's magazines also tested the waters by producing the occasional men's fashion pages. Some, such as *Queen*, before it merged with *Harper's Bazaar*, did so successfully, employing editor Erica Crome whose knowledge of the business came from many years covering fashion for *Menswear*, the trade magazine. But other stand-alone ventures floundered. *Club* magazine folded in 1970 after 21 issues, noting with some accuracy in its last issue: 'The shame is that *Club*'s closing will probably make any other publisher wary of putting out a similar product for young men.'

But while the fortunes of magazines incorporating men's fashion were mixed, mid-1960s top-shelf magazines such as *King*, *Mayfair* and *Escort* were notching up successes. Aiming to go head-on with the American import *Playboy* was *Penthouse*, headed by its formidable owner Bob Guccione who would move to New York to continue publishing and was reported by journalist Anthony Haden-Guest in *New York* magazine in February 2004 to have 'pushed the soft-core envelope building one of the most profitable porn empires in the world'.

However, the fact that there were no magazines offering fashion advice or recommendation made little difference to the impetus of the Peacock Revolution. New shops and designers were getting themselves noticed and, capitalizing on the absence of the magazines, national newspapers ran the occasional men's fashion feature or news item. Column inches were devoted to male personalities, especially actors, and the way they dressed, while music magazines such as *Rave* and publications such as *Fabulous* pictured male pop groups and pin-ups wearing cutting-edge clothing. Newspapers also charted the rise of the distinctive sub-cultures of the 1960s, as defined by fashion. Reports from the mid-1960s focused on Mods, with their fashion-obsessed cult of cool, but almost invariably referred to the financial investment made in the search for style. The *Daily Mail* recorded that one Mod 'used to go without food to buy clothes' (15 September 1964). In 1967 the *Observer Magazine* announced the demise of the Mod movement ('Ready, steady, gone') and the arrival of Flower Power. The article, which included a photo of 'flower child' Nigel Waymouth (see pp.84–9), was illustrated with a cut-out doll, which the reader was invited to dress in an Indian shirt or a raccoon coat.

In the early 1970s I joined the prestigious *Evening Standard* (editor Charles Wintour) to create the first-ever weekly newspaper column devoted to men's fashion and grooming. Following on the *Evening Standard*'s success, *The Times* also ran weekly columns. If my readers' letters were a measurement of success, it would seem these pages were appropriately timed, filling the void until a new breed of men's journals started to appear.

It was not until the late 1980s that attitudes really changed. Maybe men, as potential readers, had also changed in the intervening years. Men's magazines – both home grown and international – with pages devoted to fashion, now began to appear alongside mainstream magazines on the newsstands. Many would at last prove successful.

CHAPTER 1

The Rebirth of the Dandy

1955–63

At the end of the Second World War in 1945, Britain, like all European countries, found itself in a period of austerity. There were shortages of goods and many foods were rationed, as were clothing and petrol. In fact confectionery would be on ration until 1953. While the returning armed forces, both men and women, settled down to civilian life setting off a baby-boom, unemployment was high and the potential for young cash-strapped entrepreneurs to set up their own businesses, limited. It would take time for the country to rebuild itself and for life to return to normal.

But there were highlights as the years passed: the Festival of Britain (1951), the Coronation of Queen Elizabeth II (1953) and the conquering of Mount Everest by Edmund Hillary and his Sherpa companion, Tenzing Norgay (1953). Such events were counter-balanced by the testing of nuclear bombs by Britain and the United States (1950s–60s), while in Cuba in 1961 Fidel Castro established his socialist government.

Generally, however, the mood in London was buoyant; fun was had where it could be, especially by the young. Some argued that the 1960s became famous out of a sense of rebellion by the younger generation although, in fact, it was the late 1950s that was the seminal time. Young men were returning home fresh from National Service and finding work, and often their girlfriends were already in employment, so everyone had a little money in their pockets. The younger generation instinctively knew its time

had come. The constraints and unwelcome abstinence of earlier years had started to lift, so for them it was not so much a matter of rebelling; it was more a matter of seeking personal freedom and expression. Of living their own lives by their own standards. By the mid-1950s groups of working-class lads from London's East End had already started to show this in the way they dressed. They were the Teddy Boys.

In hand-tailored clothes that bore little resemblance to the accepted masculine mode of dress of their fathers, grandfathers or peer groups – for whom a suit might have been proudly worn for weddings, funerals and a special night out on the town – the Teds, as they became known, wore Edwardian-inspired, custom-made, long draped jackets with drainpipe black trousers. They moved in groups that looked dramatically different, a little theatrical and, always, a little threatening. They looked nothing like Mr Average and delighted in being in the public eye, accepting the nickname bestowed upon them by the national newspapers – Teddy and Ted being the diminutive forms of Edward (of the Edwardian-style jacket).

Teds' wages hovered around £8 a week and although many may have given some of this modest amount to their mothers, the remainder of their disposable incomes appears to have been put towards their appearance. The jackets were not items you could buy at multiple tailors in the high street; for these 'drapes' you

Opposite Couturier Hardy Amies outside his Savile Row salon in a suit checkered with a bitter chocolate brown always referred to as 'Hardy Amies brown'; the suit was made at Nutters, 1971. Photograph: Adrian Consolé. Hardy Amies Archive.

Above A great day of celebration as Teddy Boys strutting their distinctive finery gathered in London for the Elvis Presley fan club convention. c.1957. Photograph: David Reed/Redferns.

needed the skills of a specialist tailor. In fact the jackets were so expensive that local tailors agreed to be paid 'on tick', in instalments. But for Teds the price was worth it. Through wearing these clothes you belonged to a peer group and you stood out from the crowd. Teds did not consider themselves interested in fashion as such; they were just making a point, take it or leave it: I am who I am.

But wittingly or unwittingly, the Teds were making a fashion statement. These were clothes to be seen in, especially at weekends when, work over, you could strut your stuff on street corners and stand out with the girls at the Palais, the local dance hall with a great band and music. Their parents may have made financial sacrifices, saving money where they could for the future, but these young men were earning their own money and wanted to spend it, too. Clothes and entertainment were the priorities.

By an unlikely quirk, the inspiration for the Teds' jackets originated with the smart tailors of Savile Row, of whom few Teds would ever have heard.

In order to stimulate the revival of a dormant made-to-measure business after the war, London tailors were encouraged by the menswear trade's Dress Council to promote a return to the elegance of the Edwardian period. Savile Row's image was proving to be both an advantage and a disadvantage; an

advantage because the Row's tailors were known throughout the world for their exemplary skills but a disadvantage in that their clothes were more famous for their never-changing appearance than for their innovation. A man could wear his Savile Row suit for a decade without bowing to a trend; many did. The Council reasoned that by recreating the elegance of the Edwardian era's longer jackets, the two- or three-piece suits customarily worn by every man would be outdated.

The retro look caught on in a modest way and, for a while, dashing young bucks, officers stationed in London and younger members of the aristocracy all dressed in full Edwardiana, wearing long, narrow jackets trimmed with velvet on the lapels, brocade waistcoats and narrow trousers. Young working-class men catching sight of the Edwardian bravura saw its potential. In no time they turned it into their own expression of independence using local or East End tailors. They exaggerated its shape to good effect: shoulders were wider than Savile Row's suggestion and trousers were narrower still. In this distinctive garb they could strut about as members of an exclusive fraternity. It was a personal statement not to be ignored and, in a pack, they could be territorial and present themselves as a force to be reckoned with. This was not fancy dress, however. Nor was the man wearing it considered a dandy – the word 'dandy' would have been alien anyway. A Ted's appearance was a serious matter; it was a uniform. It made standing out as a Peacock acceptable.

Above Two decades after first appearing on London's streets, the Wembley Rock and Roll Festival in August 1972 (featuring Chuck Berry, Little Richard, Jerry Lee Lewis and Bo Diddley among others) gave Britain's Teddy Boys a joyous event to remember. Photograph: *Evening Standard/* Getty Images.

Opposite Cecil Beaton, renowned Society photographer, attached great importance to style and appearance, and embraced the Peacock movement with enthusiasm. *Evening Standard*, 24 April 1970. Photograph: Roy Jones/*Evening Standard*/Getty Images.

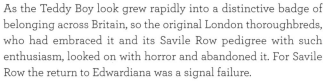

As the Teddy Boy look grew rapidly into a distinctive badge of belonging across Britain, so the original London thoroughbreds, who had embraced it and its Savile Row pedigree with such enthusiasm, looked on with horror and abandoned it. For Savile Row the return to Edwardiana was a signal failure.

To get the sartorial look right, a Ted's jacket had to be long, to the knees, and had to have generously wide shoulders to give its wearer swagger. The cut had to create a drape that was shaped inwards at the waist but still fitted comfortably. It could be black, maroon or a pale shade of blue in colour but it had to have velvet trims (preferably black), not only on the lapels but also on the collar, breast pocket and cuffs to give extra dash. Worn correctly, it was teamed with a classic white shirt, a skinny, loosely knotted tie known as a Slim Jim and a fancy waistcoat that added colourful formality. The tight black drainpipe trousers worn with the jacket had to be cut short enough to show off yellow or red socks (often knitted by a mother or sister at home). Completing the outfit only chunky crepe-soled suede slip-ons known as 'brothel creepers' would do, or, for some, sharp pointed 'winkle pickers' that had become the rage around 1957 when pointed-toe Italian shoes appeared in the shops.

Teds embraced all things American, especially rock 'n' roll. The newly arrived American music was absorbed quickly by their rebellious culture and Elvis Presley and Gene Vincent were soon their revered idols. Both were their inspiration when it came to styling hair, too. Aping their heroes, Teds applied lavish amounts of Brylcreem to the hair, which was slicked into position creating a shiny, up-thrusting quiff over the forehead and a 'D.A.' at the back. (The initials appropriately highlighted the resemblance of the combed hair to a duck's arse.) Side burns, like the evident large comb in the back pocket of the trousers, were obligatory and there to be seen. This was pure style.

Teddy Girls, too, had their own look: for preference tight black sweaters or demure blouses, worn to show off welcoming bosoms, teamed with tight toreador pants or tight black skirts and sling-back shoes, often in white. A Teddy Girl's hair was either home-permed into little curls like Connie Francis, who rose to fame in 1958 singing 'Who's sorry now', or in a ponytail. Both styles were favoured by Hollywood beach party movies.

Teds are credited with being the first social group in Britain to be identified as teenagers. Until then shops catered for pre-school and school-age children or their parents, and nothing in-between. This new market – consisting of young people fresh out of school, just in work, unmarried and, more importantly, with their own spending money – had never before been considered as a separate entity with separate needs. With the arrival of beat groups, rock 'n' roll, coffee bars, juke boxes, gramophone records, clubs and even a jargon of their own, a previously untapped world

Above Favouring tailors Watson, Fargerstrom & Hughes, couturier Neil 'Bunny' Roger cut a distinctive figure every day on his way to the Hardy Amies salon in Savile Row. Invariably he would wear frock coat, tight trousers and bowler hat, all in pale dove grey. Naturally he carried gloves and wore spats. c.1950. Photograph: Michael Boys. Hardy Amies Archive.

Above Leo Abse, a colourful backbench MP, denied he was an exhibitionist, claiming that his dandified clothes merely reflected his character. He piloted bills to reform laws on homosexuality and divorce. *Evening Standard*, 21 April 1969. Photograph: Hulton Archive/*Evening Standard*/Getty Images.

of commercial opportunity for both manufacturers and retailers, aimed exclusively at young people, was opened up.

But as Teds colonised north and north-east London , so the Mods, a middle-class teenage group, were evolving in south London and on the south coast.

All Mods (as in Modern) were followers of fashion, fixated on clothes and personal appearance, from hair to shoe. Male Mods dressed like archetypal art school students, still living at home with their parents. They were clean-cut and neatly turned out. They wore suits or sports jackets that were sometimes boxy, but more often had a nipped in waist with square shoulders, which they teamed with shirts that had long collars, neat ties and flannels. Their places of pilgrimage were the Carnaby Street shops of John Stephen (see pp.40–45) and those of his arriviste competitors (though not Vince Man's Shop (see pp.36–39) with its predominantly homosexual clientele). Writing in the *Daily Mail* on 12 February 1964, Judy Innes concluded that a male Mod's average weekly wage was between £7 10s and £10. Of this about £3 a week went on clothes. The clothes he bought cost 20 to 30 guineas for a suit, 3 guineas for a shirt and anything from 5 to 10 guineas for a pair of shoes. How did he do it? According to Innes, he saved, borrowed or starved.

It was essential for a Mod to have a scooter, or to have a friend

with one. A Lambretta or a Vespa, preferably with a fox's tail flying from an aerial fixed to the pillion seat. On their scooters they would wear anoraks with hoods trimmed with a piece of fur, or navy blue labourers' donkey jackets. Both of these were purchased at stores like Willetts, which supplied workmen's clothes and army surplus, while the fur came from moulting stoles and moth-ridden tippets that were a staple fixture at jumble sales and in second-hand shops. Apart from the fur trims, Mods were not flamboyant but neat.

Mod girls were inspired by the clothes in Mary Quant's Bazaar, though they probably shopped at places like Bus Stop or Biba, owned by Lee Bender and Barbara Hulanicki, where prices were much lower. They wore mini-skirts and ringed their eyes with black mascara. False eyelashes were available everywhere. The appearance of Twiggy in the mid-1960s epitomized their look.

Unlike the Teds who adopted a threatening stance, the Mods had a gentle image. Music and clubs were their main interests. The Beatles, dressed by Soho tailor Dougie Millings (see pp.46–7), looked like prototype Mods, as did British bands like the Rolling Stones, the Who, the Yardbirds, the Kinks and the Small Faces, whose music was played in Mod haunts, at clubs such as the Flamingo and the Marquee in Soho. Mods queued weekly outside Rediffusion's studios in Kingsway so as to be seen in the dancing audience of *Ready, Steady, Go!*, the show that by featuring a group

Above George Melly, jazz singer and author, dressed with colourful exuberance both on stage and off in a style that reflected his life and preferences. His hats were equally distinctive. Photograph: Denis Cameron/Rex Features, 1964.

Above *House & Garden* editor Peter Coats in plum velvet evening suit tall. Tall and always immaculate, he believed in propriety in a man's behaviour and dress – whatever the time of day. Photograph: Peter Rand, 1975.

or singer wearing the latest gear would spread London's newest fashion ideas across Britain.

Rockers, too, made their first appearance at this time, ex-Teds most of them, some still in their drapes although many had moved on, abandoning the Teddy Boy look for one that required a black leather jacket and a heavy motorbike. Would-be Hell's Angels, they were fuelled by a passion for rock 'n' roll, Harley-Davidsons and Marlon Brando's image of rebellion in Elia Kazan's 1954 film *On the Waterfront*, in which he wears T-shirts and jeans. For Rockers, actors like Brando and James Dean had the look, an identifiable sense of style and an undeniable sexiness that was driven by the way they dressed. Rockers were the antithesis of Mods. And this led to confrontation.

Mods and Rockers were interpreted by the clothes they wore. Rockers considered Mods weedy and effeminate because of their clean turn-out and girly motor scooters. Mods considered the Rockers coarse, badly dressed and badly behaved and, worse, grubby. Musically there was not much common ground either. Rockers listened only to rock 'n' roll by white American artists like Elvis Presley, Gene Vincent and Eddie Cochran. Mods liked British groups like the Rolling Stones and the American Motown sound. By the time the two factions faced each other in street brawls in the summer of 1964, the Mods' aesthetic leanings had been usurped by mulish elements set on becoming as violent as the Teds. When they clashed again the following year in staged confrontations in the coastal resort towns of Clacton, Brighton, Bournemouth and Margate, the newspapers headlined the clashes as riots. On each occasion there was mayhem for two days, with a number of casualties on both sides and damage to property. Then everyone went home, sated.

As the 1960s progressed so Teds, Mods and Rockers began to disappear. None of these groups could be lasting arbiters of style, nor could they become trendsetting or have fashion influence beyond their home ground: perhaps they were the wrong class.

But already lining up for their turn in the spotlight were men who would cement the legitimacy of interest in men's clothes. Most were well-born, often from noble stock, and prepared to become as self-indulgently obsessed in the way they dressed as their girlfriends. For them there was nothing wrong with standing out or looking a fop; in fact, as an idea, this was certainly agreeable. The men who were slow off the mark were either gay and therefore wary of open display, or men who would only keep up with changing times when pressured by wives and girlfriends.

In fact, this path had already been trodden by an earlier generation of dandies with an all-consuming interest in their appearance. Some made regular eye-catching public appearances, such as politician Leo Abse on Budget Day, while for entertainers like

George Melly, who added camp eccentricity to his wardrobe, the way you looked was as important as your on-stage performance. Other dandies seen daily around London were equally self-concerned but while their style was considered classical, in the manner of the Duke of Windsor, their tailors were instructed to use brighter fabrics, wider lapels and narrower trousers, to make them stand out in their peer group. Luminaries included couturier Hardy Amies, photographer Cecil Beaton and Peter Coats, the garden editor of *House & Garden*. Standing out flamboyantly gay among this courtly group was Neil Roger, a couturier who became a partner in Hardy Amies' Savile Row salon. Known to all as Bunny, he was, as Clive Fisher's obituary in the *Independent*, 29 April 1997, reported, 'a social ornament', adding that 'his 150 suits catered, albeit theatrically, for every contingency'. Sotheby's auctioned his wardrobe in January 1998.

Like their predecessors in the previous decade, Peacocks of the 1960s were swept up by a sense of liberation, wanting to enjoy life while being as little like their parents as possible. Coming from upper-class families they saw clothes as a diversion, an amusement, a pleasure, a unique way of expressing oneself. No gangs for them. Naturally, many were living on allowances from Daddy while they looked around for work.

It was from this position of confident privilege that they would stimulate the market place, giving it a fresh burst of confidence.

Their appearance as Peacocks, not least on the pages of Society magazines and national newspapers, would convince both manufacturers and retailers that the only way forward was through youthful change. The stimulus generated by their public presence would cause the spread of men's clothes shops and designer labels as well as the concept of men's hairdressing salons and a market place for grooming products that would include men's face creams and eye-bag gels. Thanks to them, men and fashion would become linked not only legitimately, but also commercially.

Endorsing the change in 1964, couturier Hardy Amies, who had been engaged two years earlier as consultant design to Hepworths, the multiple tailors, suggested that the company celebrate its centenary year by donating £20,000 to the Royal College of Art for the establishment of a menswear design department within the School of Fashion. Among the first students was Antony Price, whose 1968 collection was reminiscent of the Bisto Kids advertisements. On leaving college, he immediately became successful as a stylist and tailor to such music icons as Brian Ferry and David Bowie, just one of a whole new generation of cutting-edge, college-trained designers to enter the world of men's fashion.

Above A short white raincoat by Laurence Willcocks. In the background is Professor Janey Ironside, the iconic head of the Royal College of Art Fashion School. *The Sunday Times*, 28 March 1965. Photograph: John French/Fashion Museum, Bath.

Above The Bisto Kid look with a lean, double-breasted oak brown leather coat, soft herringbone brown tweed slouch cap and knotted brown chiffon scarf. By Antony Price for the 1968 Royal College of Art fashion show. Photograph: Peter Rand, 1968.

BILL GREEN

Vince Man's Shop

NEWBURGH STREET

On the corner of Newburgh Street and Fouberts Place, just off Carnaby Street, Vince was a small boutique with a name that brought knowing smiles to some faces and blushes to others. Its clientele was mostly theatrical and artistic (which, in this instance, meant homosexual) and its cramped changing room had a singular reputation. Jazz singer and writer George Melly is credited with being the first comedian to use the trusted joke about shopping: 'I went into there [Vince] to buy a tie and they measured my inside leg'.

The proprietor of Vince Man's Shop, to give the shop its formal name, was Bill Green, an unassuming photographer who used the nom-de-plume Vince and whose work prior to opening the shop in October 1954 concentrated exclusively on photographing muscular men. He liked them to be as near-nude as possible but, as these were still the censorious 1950s, he was compelled to cover their focal attributes modestly with tight but tiny briefs or skimpy shorts which, as he could not find anything that matched his requirements for showing the body beautiful to best effect, he created himself by cutting down regular roll-ons (also known as pantie-girdles), bought in Marks & Spencer or local shops.

When fans of his pictures began asking where they too could buy these minimal items, Green spotted a business opportunity. He placed an advertisement in the *Daily Mirror* and within a week had received orders totalling £200. This was a considerable amount in 1950 and it encouraged him to seek regular production and set up his own mail order business. Then, after a holiday in Paris where he saw young men in existentialist mode wearing black sweaters and black jeans, he added sweaters and casual slacks to his growing range of mail order clothes. More success followed so, using his photographic pseudonym to signal his presence, he opened Vince, the first boutique in the Carnaby Street neighbourhood, two years before John Stephen would set up shop and claim the territory as his own.

In the 1950s this northern corner of Soho was impoverished, an area of cramped streets alive with rag-trade warehouses and over-crowded sweatshops where tailors and seamstresses cut and sewed suits for Savile Row and shirts for Jermyn Street. A tobacconist and a handful of cafés catered for the workers' basic needs. Close to Vince were the local municipal baths, where many of Green's models were discovered, as well as being a gay haunt that would provide many future customers. Only a minute away was the London Palladium, where glamorous musicals were presented complete with numerous lithe, male dancers. Green liked clothes to be figure-hugging; so did the dancers.

Although the business seemed to satisfy a need, it had a comparatively small turnover – Green was not an experienced retailer. But he offered a broad spectrum of casual clothes none the less, such as sweaters (tight), summer slacks (form-fitting,

Opposite Carnaby Street, c.1968, open for business and proudly British. As more boutiques opened, fashion was ever-changing. Photograph: Getty Images.

often hipster) and minimal swimwear (defiantly called men's bikinis). His white polo-neck sweater became a must-have fashion item; so did the mattress-ticking casual slacks and the faded denim jeans he introduced long before faded denim became a staple of every jeans brand.

The tiny but noticeably camp corner shop had an ambivalent clientele, more heterosexual than gay according to Green. Among his celebrity clients he would list Peter Sellars, the King of Denmark and Anthony Armstrong-Jones who, Green claimed, bought his trousseau there before he married Princess Margaret.

To service his clientele Green introduced his mail order catalogue, with distinctive photographs taken by Vince. As the clothes were worn by seemingly unabashed muscular models and celebrated boxers like Billy Walker, the catalogues were something the shop's customers took home to admire in private. These were the days when the gay community was barely visible; to be seen publicly with a Vince catalogue, a man would be deemed to be queer.

The models wearing the clothes were reputed to be truck drivers, taken for the photo shoots to the Channel Islands, although actor Sean Connery, a Mr Scotland finalist in 1950, appeared in the first catalogue in 1954 and again, memorably, in an advertisement in 1957. Sitting in a sunny open-air café, decked out fetchingly in striped denim Capri shirt with tapered waist, faded blue

French-style denim jeans and stripey espadrilles with ties around the ankle, he wears movie star sunglasses to complete the outfit. Together, the shirt and jeans cost £4 6s.

Green was unaware of it at the time, but his shop was a forerunner of things to come. He was not a talented designer as such, but he brought fashion and colour to leisure clothes, making them acceptable to be worn at weekends or, as he suggested, when entertaining at home.

Due to its flamboyant contents the shop had a particular exclusivity: the clothes you found here, you were unlikely to find anywhere else. His liberation may even have been inspirational. Malcolm McLaren credits a Vince catalogue as giving him the idea for a Let It Rock shirt a decade later, and one of the shop assistants for a matter of weeks was a man with ambition and fashion flair who, on learning the trade, would move into a shop of his own in Carnaby Street and so start an empire. His name was John Stephen.

By the mid-1960s, overtaken by fierce competition, Green moved Vince out of the district to Marylebone and soon after gave up the fashion business altogether. Briefly he became a restaurateur with a restaurant in Warren Street called, with full camp implication, Auntie's. Decades after his retirement his photographic studies of he-men became collector's items. His catalogues, too.

Above Numerous pages of men in underwear considered revealing gave the Vince catalogue its racy reputation, while in the countryside men, as seen by Vince, dressed as if every day was the height of summer. 1962 catalogue. Private collection.

Opposite In the censorious 1950s the Vince catalogue was considered daringly homosexual in its content because of the abundance of photographs of muscular men wearing skimpy underwear and swimwear. 1962 catalogue. Private collection.

VINCE

99

mans shop 1962

John Stephen

CARNABY STREET

True Peacocks never dressed at John Stephen's Carnaby Street boutiques; they bought their clothes on the other side of Regent Street where the shops were smarter. By unashamedly catering for middle-class Mods, Stephen may have sold fashionable clothes at a lesser price, but they came with less cachet; Carnaby Street could never be Peacock territory. However, it was Stephen's impact on Britain's dormant world of men's clothing that sent liberating ripples outwards on a national scale and affected more than just a small, youthful pocket of middle-class men. In 1964 the *Daily Sketch* called him 'The Apostle of the Mods of our time' and with a certain amount truth Stephen was able to claim, 'There was no fashion for men and then we came along.'

John Stephen was a young, slender, good-looking Glaswegian who, shy though he was, liked standing out in a crowd. He had an infectious, consuming passion for clothes and by the age of 26 he had brought fame and bustling life to the narrow, drab roads behind Regent Street's quintessentially British department stores of Liberty and Jaeger, the smart French store Galleries Lafayette and London's landmark toy shop, Hamleys. His arrival rescued an area of Soho that until then was both neglected and impoverished. It was here that he provided Mods with the clothes they wanted.

Like Mary Quant, whose first shop Bazaar opened in 1955 in the King's Road less than a year before Stephen's own first shop made

its mark, John Stephen and his Carnaby Street creation are indelibly fixed as proof of the Swinging Sixties experience. When New York journalists, reporting in the 1960s on London's street fashions, declared that the capital's boutique-based designers were the most important and imaginative force in world fashion, Stephen's empire endorsed their convictions.

Stephen arrived in London from Scotland in 1952. He was 18 and found work as a salesman at £6 a week in the military department of Moss Bros in Covent Garden, which was then a gentleman's outfitter as well as eminent tailor of both military and state uniforms. The staid atmosphere of the company did not appeal to him but he lasted four years before working, briefly, for Bill Green in his camp boutique Vince (see p.36–9).

Working at Vince proved inspirational and led Stephen and his partner Bill Franks to strike out independently by opening their own small shop called His Clothes on the first floor of premises in neighbouring Beak Street, at No.19. They had limited finances, which meant limited quantities of stock, so they began with items similar to Vince's best-sellers. Like lilac shirts and pink denim jeans. In this unlikely location a young clientele developed. As success beckoned, Stephen's obsession with carving a prominent place in menswear took over. He craved fame, affluence and recognition; with Mods now appearing on his street, retailing seemed the perfect route to achievement.

Opposite Members of aspiring bands like the Pirates were typically sent to Stephen's boutiques to be kitted out in the latest fashions by their record labels. The single-breasted white cotton jacket was a classic favourite. *The Sunday Times*, 6 June 1965. Photograph: Mike McGrath/Fashion Museum, Bath.

Above John Stephen on home ground in 1968. The Glaswegian catalyst had become the uncrowned king of Carnaby Streets, 1968. Photograph: Colin Davey/Camera Press.

When fire destroyed all his stock in 1956, Stephen found the impetus he needed. The duo moved into an empty shop at 5 Carnaby Street, with a window in which to display merchandise, at a fixed rent of £7 a week. The timing was right. With his arrival the ever-increasing Mods found clothes ripe for purchase, colourfully presented. At the back of the boutique a handful of tailors and seamstresses turned new designs into reality in a cramped workshop. Until then confirmed Mods often had their clothes made to measure locally by outworkers making items for West End shops. Even if Stephen's future customers had known they wanted such a vast array of ready-made clothes, they would have found them impossible to find.

'When we first started we didn't think about success,' said Bill Franks in 2009, recalling those heady days. 'We just started. We were having fun. We had so little money that when we took over the first shop all we could do was paint the shop front canary yellow, so it stood out in the dreary back streets, and make the fixtures and fittings ourselves from old orange boxes, which we covered in felt.'

'We started manufacturing almost immediately but had such limited stock, one of each style, that when a customer bought something we had to have another one made immediately to replace it. In those days the whole of Soho was manufacturing clothing. You could have anything made in the tiny workrooms in those dingy streets. You could also find anything you wanted – trimmings, linings, materials, buttons, embroidery.'

Stephen claimed his success was due to being the same age as his customers and certainly his strengths appear to be a youthful drive and energy, as well as a belief in his own understanding of his burgeoning male clientele. His shyness masked determination. But, as Bill Franks now explains, 'John was passionate about doing menswear. He was miles ahead of everyone in design and ideas. He was a visionary and knew instinctively what young men wanted. Other retailers coming onto the scene just watched what he was doing and copied him. When we started, he had the youth market all to himself.'

Stephen also understood the demands of the times. As the 1950s turned into the 1960s, new clothes needed to look sophisticated even if they were destined for young men, many still teenagers, with little money to spend. Due to the Mod movement it had become acceptable for young men to be interested in fashion and spend time and money on appearances. They wanted suits and jackets – in the 1960s dressing-up still meant a touch of formality – and it was not unusual for some Stephen fans, bitten by the fashion bug, to buy a shirt a week. None wanted to look like middle-class men going to work. Or bank managers, or dull but wealthy company directors or, indeed, their fathers. These Mods, peacocks-in-the-making, wanted to look flamboyantly right, going out with – or in search of – a pretty girl, dollied up with bobbed hair, layers of black mascara and a mini skirt only a little deeper than a curtain pelmet.

Stephen wanted his customers to appear sexy; so did they. How else did you attract the girl you wanted? At the start of the fun, liberated 1960s, sexy meant showing off. The clothes proclaimed: Look at me. 'Men,' Stephen told me, 'shop for pleasure.'

The man Stephen was dressing was skinny and had never heard of pectoral muscles or gym workouts. As Franks pointed out: 'The average waist of trousers we sold was 28inch. Weren't we all 28inch in those days? If you were 32inch, you were big. Nowadays 38inch is considered normal.'

So, to dress these slender men, he updated traditional styles by slimming the fit and changing the fabric slightly. If a suit was in a Prince of Wales check, for example, it might look traditional but the jacket would have wide lapels and fit tightly, shaped at the waist, with two deep vents at the back. Its armholes would be high, the sleeves narrow. And the fabric, probably lightweight and found in a range destined for women's fashion, would have an unusual, fine line of colour running through the check.

Shirts, too, were tight and made with soft high collars that were often button-down or tab. They came in a wide variety of colours and prints, again in fabrics associated with women's dresses as well as crinkled cotton crepons, soft seersuckers and striped cotton Oxfords. For a brief period there were shirts with fly-fronts concealing the buttons.

Nothing was garish, however. Stephen's reference points were still traditional clothes worn by traditional gentlemen. He also introduced variety: large floppy shirt collars cut like spaniel-ears and a wide range of Kipper ties. (Michael Fish, who is credited with creating Kipper ties while working at Turnbull & Asser, also worked briefly for Stephen before setting up Mr Fish – see pp.104–17.)

As for trousers, he revolutionized the fit. Until then, most were baggy and held up by braces (suspenders). His patterns were cut so the trousers fitted the seat and when he introduced the world's first hipster trousers with a low rise and an even tighter fit that was both revealing and sexy, men rushed in to buy them. So did women. Within weeks hipsters appeared in other small boutiques; they had become mainstream items of clothing.

Price was a key factor of success. Stephen believed every item had to be sold competitively – meaning inexpensively. Weekly wages were low; annual pay increases were not the norm. But, with pay packets safely stashed in their pockets, great numbers of a new breed of young shopper would emerge on Saturdays, looking for the latest gear, and every week Stephen planned to provide

them with fresh ideas. So while partner Franks, in his role as chairman of the company, concentrated on the commercial aspects, that is, pricing the goods, Stephen instinctively sought to create items that would sell. Paring their profits, the average price of a jacket was less than £10, a pair of trousers £4. This was less than high street shops were charging for clothes without the Stephen kudos or eye for fashion.

Through Stephen's endeavour Carnaby Street was transformed into a trendy place for young people to meet and be seen. Music blared from the boutiques (until then shopping was a serious experience) and musicians from the new beat groups, who then earned little more than their teenage fans, also thronged the Street. What the groups bought, the fans bought too. So did young movie stars, scions of aristocratic families and young people excitedly arriving on a day trip.

Such was the resounding effect Carnaby Street was having on the world of men's clothes that a television programme was broadcast in November 1966, *A Tale of Two Streets*, in which Carnaby Street was compared to Savile Row. The Row's tailors protested, claiming that it damaged their image and presented Savile Row as an exclusive place interested only in dressing the aristocracy. 'The snobbery displayed in the programme was absurd,' squawked Anthony Sinclair, a tailor based in Conduit Street, to the *Evening Standard* in a letter quoted by Angus McGill on 30 November

1966. 'If a barrow boy wants a Savile Row suit, and can pay for it, we will make him one and very good he'll look in it too.'

Bill Franks now challenges accusations levied at the time that quality was sometimes compromised.

Nonsense. It was a million times better than people say. John used to say it worried him how long the clothes lasted! For a start cloths and raw materials were better then than they are today, when everything is imported as cheaply as possible from the Far East. And all our machinists were all properly trained. One of our top machinists had been trained sewing cardboard together for six months before being allowed to work on fabric – that's how strict some apprenticeships were. Those were the sorts of people we employed.

You could always buy small quantities of good fabric then, too, so you could keep changing what was in the shops. Sales reps called in with wonderful lengths to choose from. And there was always a machinist in Soho who could do excellent work for you. The facilities were all there.

As Carnaby Street changed from a quiet side street into a street of fashion, boutiques with names like Lord John (owned by Warren Gold, who, like Stephen, envisioned a chain of boutiques), Topper Shoes, the Carnaby Cavern and I Was Lord Kitchener's

Above Phil May and John Weider of the Pirates were dressed by John Stephen for the *Sunday Times*. For them there were three-button, single - or double - breasted, formal jackets in tweed and seersucker, as well as casual shirts. *The Sunday Times*, 6 June 1965. Photograph: Mike McGrath/Fashion Museum, Bath.

Valet opened. One boutique, Lady Jane, won remarkable national publicity by putting live models, wearing the dresses, in the shop window and was fined £2 in court for causing a disturbance.

In time, John Stephen had 15 shops spread along the length of Carnaby Street under various names – His, Mod Male, Domino Male and Male W.1. – as well as three stores on the King's Road and a small one at 159 Regent Street. Following a grand tour of the United States, during which he appeared on countless television stations, Stephen soon had 40 boutiques within American department stores. Similar outlets were opened in Canada and Europe. He seemed on track to achieving his goal: to own more shops than anyone else.

Stephen's most challenging competitor was Irvine Sellar, a retailer of great skill. He had the idea – a first in its day – of starting a chain of boutiques where both men and women could buy their clothes and where, if necessary, they would queue for the same changing room. He called the 24 boutiques Mates.

As the 1970s progressed, Britain's high street stores joined in the pursuit of younger customers with a taste for fashion, many of the stores targeting the children of their established, regular clientele. They offered 'young fashion' departments where the quality of the clothes was better than those on Carnaby Street, where standards had begun to slide. The Street's appeal was evaporating. Once a fashion centre, it was now a tourist destination, as popular as Madame Tussauds and the Tower of London. Carnaby Street's fashion moment was over.

As Franks said with understatement: 'By 1960, when we were up and running, we didn't think we'd achieved anything in particular. We just started opening one shop after another. But we were very stretched; we expanded too quickly.' Taking stock of the changing face of the fashion industry, Stephen and Franks realized it was time to move on and become a supplier rather than a retailer. A factory was set up in Glasgow and a contract signed with Rex Trueform, a South African manufacturer with a worldwide export network. Then, in 1972 the John Stephen company went public, but it soon began to run at a loss and within four years newspaper columns reported that the company was in deep trouble. Stephen resigned on health grounds. The company was bought by Raybeck, owners of several chains of high street fashion shops that coincidentally also owned the Lord John chain, which had emerged as one of Stephen's earliest rivals. When Raybeck itself was taken over in 1986, the John Stephen brand name vanished.

On Stephen's death in 2004 Bill Franks donated the John Stephen archive to the Victoria and Albert Museum, London. In 2005 a plaque was unveiled in John Stephen's honour in Carnaby Street, endorsing what Nik Cohn, author and journalist, wrote in *Today There Are No Gentlemen*: 'He was hardly a designer, he was a moment'.

Above Lord Snowdon and Princess Margaret on honeymoon in Sardinia, May 1965. Snowdon's single-breasted, four-button, linen jacket with patch pockets, was 10 gns at John Stephen. Photograph: Rex Features.

Dougie Millings

OLD COMPTON STREET

One of the definitive images of the Beatles was captured in a photograph taken in December 1962, in which the youthful, fresh-faced group have pudding-basin haircuts and wear elegantly tailored suits with tightly buttoned, but collarless, formal jackets. Responsible for this sartorial look was Dougie Millings, a budding tailor working from a cutting-room in the heart of Soho, at 63 Old Compton Street. By chance this new-look jacket had been promoted in Paris earlier, in 1960, by Pierre Cardin, whose seasonal collections had begun to stimulate international interest in men's fashion. Only a cynic would disbelieve Millings when he denied he was influenced by Cardin. But coincidence or not, Millings redefined the way Britain's performers dressed. He was now in business big-time.

Born in 1913 in Manchester, Millings trained initially as a bespoke tailor at Leith Academy in Edinburgh. After short periods of apprenticeship in Edinburgh and Leeds, he arrived in London in the 1930s to work as a cutter at Hector Powe, a gentlemen's outfitters in Regent Street known particularly for tailoring military uniforms for serving officers. By 1952 he had taken over the tailoring facilities at Austins in Shaftsbury Avenue and six years later, striking out again but this time on his own, he moved into Soho where he shared a first-floor cutting-room with another tailor.

It was an auspicious move. Among his early clients was Tito Burns, who had discovered Dusty Springfield and was then managing Cliff Richard. To give the fledgling Richard a rock 'n' roll image, Millings created a dramatic white suit. The singer's success grew and Millings was soon dressing other rock luminaries. Among them were Billy Fury (in a gold lamé suit, 1961), Bill Hailey and the Comets (in plaid jackets, 1958) and Roy Orbison (in black suits with zip-fronted jackets, 1963).

Then, in 1962, Brian Epstein brought in the Beatles for a make-over, having seen his other group – Gerry and the Pacemakers – dressed by Millings. The resulting collarless jackets made history. Their design and workmanship were such that Millings was soon making suits for the Beatles' private lives, as well as professional outfits for their tours and the films *A Hard Day's Night* (1964) and *Help!* (1965).

His ensuing fame encouraged Millings to expand and he moved to grander premises in Great Pulteney Street, where his show biz client list grew to include Sammy Davis Jnr, Warren Beatty, Steve McQueen, the Rolling Stones, the Everly Brothers, the Temptations and the Who. In 2000, a year before he died, he was quoted in *GQ* (April 2000) as saying that Keith Moon of the Who 'died in one of my suits. In fact, he hadn't paid for it.'

In 1983, aged 70 and with decades of tailoring behind him, Millings closed his large premises but continued to work for private clients.

Opposite The Beatles in the collarless suits popularized by tailor Dougie Millings (centre) in 1962, which instantly cast the Fab Four's international image. 1962. Photograph: Harry Hammond.

Above Pierre Cardin introduced collarless suits in his first major men's fashion collection in 1960. With its space age imagery, it was known as the Cylinder Look. Photograph: Keystone.

CHAPTER 2

Men's Fashion and the 1960s

1960-69

Men's fashion not only arrived during the 1960s, it also grew up. Embraced by talented, sometimes precocious, personalities from the arts world, pursuing the stamp of the individual in their appearance as well as their work, the door that had been pushed opened by the first wave of 'anything goes' boutiques in Carnaby Street now led the way to smart men's clothing shops in the West End and the King's Road. They even invaded the inner sanctum of Savile Row. And here, tailors, renowned for elegant but traditional gentleman's clothing, also began to cater for younger, more fashion-conscious customers, as did the more mainstream department stores. As the decade progressed, men's clothing became more about fashion and less a statement about social revolution. The dressing-up box was quietly put away.

In February 1960 the Society magazine *Queen* (proprietor Jocelyn Stevens with editor Beatrix Miller, who would steer British *Vogue* through decades of success) ran a feature titled 'The 20 Most Eligible Men' for their upmarket readers. Many of the men, as you might expect of such a magazine, had an aristocratic title and dressed expensively, using the cream of London's Savile Row tailors and getting their shirts made to measure in Jermyn Street. Among them were the Duke of Atholl, Viscount Chelsea, Angus Ogilvy and Billy Wallace, all names long associated in the national press with the possession of bags of money and grand estates, with royal connections and serial nightclubbing with the pretty Princess Margaret. Clement Freud, raconteur and journalist,

quipped that Miller's targeted reader of this kind of non-essential information was a Society girl named Caroline who had long hair, had left school at the age of 16, was not bright, but was the sort of person that one ended up in bed with. Had *Queen* repeated this feature two years later for Caroline and her chums, the cast of eligible men would have changed. London's social scene had moved on.

The key to the 1960s was the pursuit of personal liberation, subconscious or otherwise; the pursuit of the best life could offer. For the first time within memory neither class nor social background mattered as incomes rose with entrepreneurial freedom, and revived job creation centred on a youth market that was willing to work as it sought to improve its lifestyle. It was a time of enterprise-friendly opportunity and expansion. Unlike their parents whose lives were enshrined in class tradition, this generation found it possible to move unhindered between class and social groupings. There were no apparent barriers. Everyone was confident that life would be more interesting, if not better, than it was for his or her parents. It never occurred to them it could be otherwise.

An alternative culture ushered in 1960s novelties like hippie communes, Indian gurus and meditation, Italian restaurants and pizzas, and changes in attitudes to sex and drugs. The advent of the contraceptive pill facilitated social change. Poet Philip Larkin

Opposite David Hockney, artist, in handmade woollen sweater with parrot artwork. Similar sweaters were knitted with faces, from Groucho Marx to Donny Osmond, while tongue-in-cheek versions could be commissioned from Betty Barnden who would knit your portrait. One man chose his dog. Photograph: Jonathan Moore, 1974. Private collection.

Above Dr Roy Strong in 1968, then director of the National Portrait Gallery, was known for his interest in clothes and making a dapper appearance wherever he went. The Fashion Museum in Bath displays 16 of his shirts and matching ties from the 1960s to 1990s. Photograph: Fashion Museum, Bath.

famously wrote in his poem *Annus Mirabilis* (1967): 'Sexual intercourse began in 1963'. For the generation taking over London 'sex, drugs and fashion' might have been more appropriate. Young people were breaking down barriers in moral attitudes and social habits and showed their independence outwardly through the way they dressed. Everyone under 35 and living in London was aware, if not influenced, by the changes brought on by the modernizing mood.

In these uninhibited years, only talent and energy seemed to matter although appearances – that is, dressing well and being groomed – mattered, too. As magazines, newspapers and television expanded their coverage, so looking good took on more importance. Books were written about it. More than ever, it was an essential ingredient of success. A new breed of young entrepreneurs emerged. Men's fashion became a legitimate business.

With the lean postwar years only a dim recollection, London itself was revitalized and while having fun was a priority, ambition in itself was not a questionable trait. Many aspiring to own the town were prepared to take great risks forging ahead, if not exactly challenging the Establishment, then ignoring all it stood for. As new business flourished, London turned into the most uninhibited and gayest (in the old sense of the word: lively) city in the world. As was said at the time, London was where the action was.

Many claims are made for the first person to use the term Swinging London. *Time* magazine lays claim to the honour for a feature that appeared on 15 April 1966, pointing to *London: the Swinging City*. But this was merely confirmation of what had already gone before. The first person was probably anglophile Diana Vreeland, American *Vogue*'s great New York editor and fashion seer, who had declared a year earlier that 'London is the most swinging city in the world at the moment'. Or maybe the honour should go to another American journalist, John Crosby, who at roughly the same time, April 1965, put the words into print. Writing in Britain's *Weekend Telegraph* magazine he claimed, 'London is the most exciting city in the world', defining it further as a happening place where youth ruled and anything goes. It was, he wrote, 'absolutely Swinging'.

In his feature Crosby particularly highlighted the apparent revolution in men's clothes. These were the days when it was not unusual to see men in the City wearing bowler hats (the best coming from James Lock & Co. in St James, founded in 1676 and still going strong) and swinging a Swaine, Adeney & Brigg umbrella. He wrote:

[The revolution] is very much part of the London swinging scene, partly because it's adding so much dash and colour and glamour to the London Street scene, but also as a sign of deeper social turmoil that is transforming England ... English men's clothes

Opposite The Hon. Tara Browne, dressed by his wife Nicky in double-breasted maroon silk suit from Major Hayward with a Turnbull & Asser gold-coloured shirt for *Men in Vogue*, November 1966. Photograph: Michael Cooper.

Above Christopher Gibbs, antique dealer and arbiter of style in 1966. His shopping guide in *Men in Vogue* described the best, most beautiful, extraordinary and wearable clothes in the shops. Photograph: Terrence Spencer/Time Life Pictures/Getty Images.

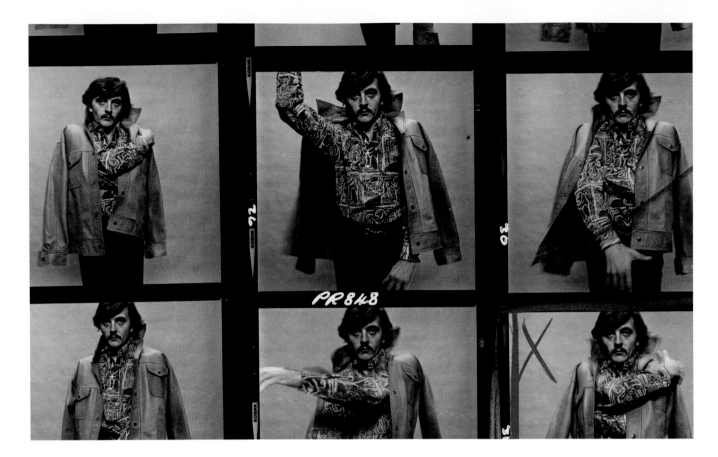

were once almost uniform: staid, sober and, above all, correct, advertising your precise rung on the social ladder and even your bank account. Today the working-class boys – many of them fresh out of the Army or Navy and in full revolt against conformity of dress – their pockets full of money, are splurging on suede jackets, skin-like trousers, double-breasted pin-striped suits (the very latest mode) with two buttons – or perhaps six. The impact of Carnaby Street is becoming worldwide.

Getting into his stride, Crosby then identified the Peacocks and their separate class:

The same thing on a different social and income level can be seen at Blades where the custom-made suits cost £52. At Blades the clothes have an elegance and a sort of look-at-me dash not seen since Edwardian times. On the racks I found, just as an example of what goes on there, a jet black velvet dinner jacket – trousers the same material – with a mandarin collar and buttons that I would never have the courage to wear.

What he had happened on were small groups of clothes-conscious young men making a truly visual impact as they moved unhindered in the new London between the overlapping worlds of fashion, advertising, theatre, the arts, media and social class. Smart London was dressing up. If a man owned a Blades velvet suit, he wore it with casual aplomb.

The same class of people who had adorned the pages of *Queen* were still around town, but the Peacocks among London's new breed of 'beautiful people' (as the tabloid press referred to them) now wore less formal, more relaxed, clothes bought at the latest smart places. These were far removed both in attitude and taste from the hallowed confines of Savile Row and Jermyn Street although even here, it has to be said, concerned tailors and shirt-makers were already wondering how to tap into the rich lode of the evolving, younger, fashion-conscious market. First off the mark was the shirt-maker Turnbull & Asser which, in 1967, famously distanced itself from competition with the Street's other shirt shops by introducing ready-made shirts in a wide variety of colours and fabrics, many of them totally washable in spun, woven silks made by its own factory. Until that momentous event, every shirt in Jermyn Street was bespoke, that is, made-to-measure.

For Peacocks being 'cool' meant dressing more casually than was customary. This often led to confrontation in restaurants where, in the continuing manner of the Establishment's gentlemen's clubs dotted around Pall Mall, pre-1960s dress codes were adhered to and the manager would present a tie to any man who deigned to walk in without one. (For this eventuality a number of unattractive narrow ties that no one would consider stealing were kept behind the reception desk.) Falling foul of this rule, in 1962 Lord Snowdon arrived at Mario & Franco's highly fashionable Trattoria Terrazza in Soho decked out in a jacket but wearing a polo-neck shirt,

Above and opposite David Hemmings, actor and star of such films as *Blow Up* and *The Charge of the Light Brigade*, in reversible leather and suede biker jacket, £27 at Harrods, teamed with Batik over-printed blue Madras shirt, £3, by Peter Golding. Photograph: Peter Rand.

purchased at trendsetting Turnbull & Asser, and found he was denied entry. Only when Franco – or was it Mario? – interceded to explain fashion's newest trend, did his partner let Snowdon in.

With symbols of tribal loyalties like old school or regimental ties now abandoned, these men looked exactly like the crowds of a very different class mix, which they joined in the trendy discotheques that now took over from nightclubs. Places with names like the Ad Lib, Scotch, Sibylla's and the Garrison, where they danced to the Beatles, the Rolling Stones, the Animals, Petula Clark and all the latest Motown stars rather than Frank Sinatra, Rosemary Clooney, Andy Williams or Tony Bennett. Those with money, fame or connections headed for Annabel's in Berkeley Square, where the ambiance was grander but the social mix much the same. Wherever they chose to be, they would be accompanied by pretty partners, in skimpy skirts with skinny legs encased in pale tights, who looked like models. Many were.

Soho coffee bars, art-house cinemas showing the cream of French and Italian films, boutiques with an abundance of leggy dollies and Chelsea's buzzing King's Road, which had turned into a daily fashion parade with a great spectacle on Saturday afternoons, all added flavour to the capital. As did the arrival of beat groups from the North.

These were the opportune years, free of constraints, and a new

breed of energetic men and women, with not a single, diluted drop of aristocratic blood between them and not much money but ready to work and play, had taken up residence. For them London was the centre of the universe.

Here were maverick talents with names to conjure with: photographers David Bailey, Terence Donovan, Brian Duffy, Norman Eales, Michael Cooper, David Montgomery; art gallery entrepreneurs Kasmin, Robert Fraser, John Dunbar; artists David Hockney and Patrick Procktor; antique dealer Christopher Gibbs, seeker out of the beautiful and curious; actors Peter O'Toole, Albert Finney, Richard Harris, Richard Burton, James Fox, Terence Stamp, Michael York; pop stars Adam Faith, Paul Jones, Eric Burdon; and a small handful of celebrity footballers headed by Bobby Moore and George Best. The girls included Julie Christie, Jean Shrimpton, Vanessa Redgrave, Susanna York, Marianne Faithfull and Charlotte Rampling.

The change in attitudes to class was apparent in British films, too. These had moved on from being charmingly domestic with 'the nobs' talking in clipped accents and now reflected the social order and mores of the time. Fine examples of British grit included *A Taste of Honey* (Shelagh Delaney, 1961), *The Loneliness of the Long Distance Runner* (Tony Richardson, 1962), *This Sporting Life* (Lindsay Anderson, 1963) and *The Servant* (Joseph Losey, 1963), while bringing the world to an apparent standstill were films like

Above Brian Jones of the Rolling Stones dressed by Anita Pallenberg in double-breasted black suit striped with red and white. Loafers from Carnaby Street. *Men in Vogue,* November 1966. Photograph: Michael Cooper.

Opposite Patrick Lichfield, photographer and courtier, bravely overdressed for a fashion magazine by Mr Fish. Beneath the evening jacket with embroidered facings the silk shirt is abundantly trimmed with a fulsome ruff, knotted with flamboyant scarf. 22 July 1971. Photograph: Associated Newspapers/Rex Features.

Darling (John Schlesinger, 1965) and *The Knack ... And How to Get It* (Richard Lester, 1965). David Lean's *Lawrence of Arabia* went on general release in 1962 as well as *Dr No* (Terence Young), the first of six James Bond movies to appear during the decade. Tony Richardson's very British film adaptation, *Tom Jones*, appeared the following year.

While Mary Quant, Ossie Clark, Sally Tuffin and Marion Foale, Jean Muir, Bill Gibb and others blazed the way with clothes for women that were young, colourful, sexy and expensive, men showed they were also ready for change. (Both Jean Muir and Bill Gibb would introduce knitwear for men in the 1970s.) The Mods had led the way, being fed instant, inexpensive fashion by John Stephen who, with his visionary commercial acumen, had centred his burgeoning boutique empire on Soho's Carnaby Street and made it their home. But an explosion of small smart shops and boutiques had began to pepper London's West End, Knightsbridge and Chelsea and these were the names that would bring fashion-conscious authority to the period. Boutiques proliferated as fast as would-be designers multiplied. These were the shops that would create and stock clothes a man could wear to show off his liberation, clothes that by the standards of the day were (mostly) simply expensive good taste. By the time the Peacock Revolution was underway, there was nothing suspect about a man wearing a velvet suit, frilly-fronted shirt or a flowing scarf tied around his neck as if emulating an eighteenth-century fop.

John Taylor, magazine editor of *Tailor & Cutter*, the menswear trade's required reading, attributed the changes to the changed attitudes to sex. 'It's simple,' he said, 'men want to look younger and more attractive. England is not such a man's world as it was.'

Men in Vogue disagreed. 'The hand that rocked the cradle is at last having some influence on the droopy fawn cardigan and the grey socks round the ankle. The Englishman's view that to be at all dandified is effete – or worse – is changing. After-shave lotions are established, deodorants a necessary commonplace and colognes are catching on.'

Angus McGill recalls his early days commentating on men's clothes in the *Evening Standard*.

When I inherited the Mainly for Men column in 1966 I got to thinking about the way men dressed for special occasions in foreign parts and became quite glum. It seemed to me that only the Chinese in their dire Mao uniforms did it worse than us.

On the other hand India cheered me up a bit. The most minor rajah in his silks and jewels, not to mention the magnificent state elephant at his gate, put the grandest city gent to shame. The three-piece suit, the collar and tie, the bowler hat, Mr Wilson in his new Gannex coat. Good grief ...

Above and opposite Louis Stanbury of Kilgour, French & Stanbury, Savile Row in 14 oz worsted suit, £80. Jacket with braided collar and cuffs, covered buttons and inverted pleats. Waistcoat in raw Indian silk. 'A bespoke suit is always individually styled and in good taste,' he said. 'Clothes are handmade by craftsmen.' *Town*, August 1967. Photograph: Peter Rand.

But as he wrote those words, thousands of virtually identical three-button, single-breasted suits were being made to varying standards of quality by Burtons, other big national chains, West End department stores and the gilded fraternity in Savile Row. McGill then gave details of what would replace them. The new suit, he reported, would have a jacket that looked like a hunting jacket, which fitted tightly across the shoulders, had small armholes and tight sleeves, and was nipped in at the waist. The trousers, he said, would be absolutely straight. In other words, the fit generally would be slimmer and tighter. More youthful.

Gauging the times two years later, the normally staid *Daily Telegraph* headlined a feature in their colour supplement, dated 5 April 1968, 'The End of the Saggy Baggy Elephant – nothing sissy about fashion for men'. My accompanying text claimed the new look was the result of the demand for less formal clothes. 'Years ago there was little call for casual wear: it was a six-day week and best clothes on Sunday. Now everything casual, as well as being easier to wear, can look formal – the roll neck shirt with a dinner jacket is a perfect example.' Viewed decades later, the feature appears to smugly pontificate although at the time it satisfied the demand for a confirmation of style. 'There are no special rules for what clothes should look like, but there are very definite recommendations,' it continued. 'Style is very much the way a person wears his clothes, the touches he adds. Beau Brummell said: If John Bull turns to look after you, you are not well-dressed but either too stiff, too tight or too fashionable.' The accompanying photographs show men dressed by Peacock favourites: Blades (see pp.94–103) and Mr Fish (see pp.104–17).

The following week's feature was headlined 'Beginning of the Rainbow – after a century under suspicion colours in men's clothes has lost its bohemian context'. My accompanying text claimed that colour had come back into men's fashion and gone was the day when the foreigner's idea of British men, held for a hundred years, was that they all looked like yards of tweed surrounded by thick fog. And taking a bolder step on 19 April, the headline read, 'When a woman's biggest rival is her husband', suggesting that men and women were now dressing in competition. To prove the point photographs by Bill King showed actor-turned-singer Anthony Newley with his wife, the actress Joan Collins; Christie's art expert William Mostyn Owen with his wife, the writer Gaia Servadio; Israeli singing duo of 'Cinderella Rockafella' fame, Abi and Esther Ofarim; and the ubiquitous society favourites, Rupert Lycett Green and his wife, Candida Betjeman. Again the men's clothes came from Blades, Mr Fish and Turnbull & Asser. The women's clothes were uncredited.

By the early 1970s the *Evening Standard* had a regular weekly column, written by myself, devoted to men and fashion, as did *The Times*, contributed by Anthony King-Deacon. Men's fashion had come of age.

Overleaf, pages 58–59 Simon Boyle of Allsopp, Brindle & Boyle, King's Road. Suit in beige whipcord, 50gns. 'We seem to dress anyone, from actors and pop-singers to parsons.' *Town*, August 1967. Photograph: Peter Rand.

PR779

The shop that previewed the Peacock trail on the eve of the 1960s was John Michael. Located at 170 King's Road, midway between Mary Quant's catalytic boutique, Bazaar, and the Woolworth's emporium, and alongside Sydney Smith's, Chelsea's premier gentlemen's outfitter, it added the next important ingredient to the street's fertile retail soil: trendy clothes for men. Coming from a family of menswear retailers, its proprietor John Michael Ingram understood exactly how to approach men's fashion and, with little competition to consider, he introduced clothes that were quietly innovative in design, neither brash nor brazen. His were the good-taste clothes of the day.

Ingram had no plans to attract Carnaby Street's Mods. Nor did he consider that flamboyant upscale Peacocks might be in the making. His commercial eye was fixed firmly on men who wanted to be offered items that looked individual without Carnaby Street's predilection for over-design and superfluous detail. He believed that his customers would want to dress neatly and colourfully, as he did, and that like him, they would be between 20 and 30, though age, as he often claimed, was of secondary importance: 'Some people are born old and won't accept anything different'.

Ingram's shop was upper middle-class in outlook and ambiance. Coming upon it for the first time was like reaching an oasis. His underlying intention was to make formal clothes more casual. And smarter. And within a few months of opening, word had spread:

John Michael clothes had the design factor that made them stand out. The shop became the place where media folk and advertising and public relations agency executives with spending power would buy the all-important clothes that would set them apart from their clients and business rivals. For them, wearing John Michael clothes showed you were in touch with happening design; they were worn, unmistakably, with pride. The clothes were expensive and unlike anything else currently on sale. In his autobiography *Stoned* (2000), the Rolling Stones' manager Andrew Loog Oldham records: '[John Michael] was a fashion plate we could ill afford but we badly wanted. I did starve a little for the superlative skinny wool knit tie and gingham tab-collared tie'.

In an interview with journalist Nik Cohn for his 1971 book *Today There Are No Gentlemen*, Ingram is quoted as saying, 'I created the middle road in male fashion. Before John Michael the only choice was between boredom on the one hand and fancy dress on the other. There was no sensible compromise'. He continued, 'Gee was fun and important but basically bad taste. I tried to get the same excitement but without the vulgarity'.

The boredom he referred to was stocked by the average high street shop; the fancy dress reference was his denigrating slant on Cecil Gee's success and his splendidly brazen, over-enthusiastic shop in Charing Cross Road that dressed everyone in show biz, as well as the flashily brave, in the latest, boldest,

Above and opposite Colin Hammick of Huntsman, Savile Row. His suit is made of a lightweight grey worsted dogstooth check with fine blue overcheck, 95gns. Jacket is one button with soft rolling lapel. 'The whole point of a bespoke suit,' he said, 'is that it always makes you look better, whoever you are.' *Town*, August 1967. Photograph: Peter Rand.

brashest and often dazzling clothes of the late 1950s. It was not for nothing that the small but seriously imposing Gee was known as Mr Swish.

Gee, however, was a talented retailer. He opened the first of his dozen shops in the East End in 1928 but soon shifted his focus to the West End, where customers might have more money. Before the Second World War and the arrival of American servicemen on British shores, he was heavily influenced by the American Look, which he interpreted as images of Hollywood's bad men: broad-shouldered gangster jackets, pleated pants and hand-painted flashy ties. By 1956, after a trip to Italy, he favoured the Italian Look – natural-shouldered, sleek, three-button jackets with short vents, narrow ties, pointed shoes – which he launched in his impressive Shaftsbury Avenue store. More influences followed and later his sons were to run a chain of shops bearing his name. They also acquired those retail outlets of the Establishment, Moss Bros in Covent Garden and the Savoy Tailor's Guild, among others.

The Ingram design team (Tom Gilbey would be among them, see page 118–23) produced clothes that were in good taste, in colours far quieter in tone than those seen in Carnaby Street. Even in his more sporty shop, Sportique, Ingram would take traditional items and reshape them without adding gimmicky detailing. He introduced ready-made, relaxed lightweight suits, pale coloured cotton seersucker jackets, and a wide range of Oxford shirts with button-down or tab collars. Summer slacks came in a variety of soft colours. In retrospect, most items were fine examples of America's preppy look.

Talking to Rodney Bennett-England for his book *Dress Optional* (1967), Ingram said: 'Carnaby Street is a different social phenomenon entirely ... It caters for a type who was working class [and it] has not so much to do with fashion as the social revolution [taking place]. Most of their manufacturers and shops are making too much of an effort. There is only one ambition – to do something more peculiar than the next one. It all has a short-term validity'.

As it happened most of Ingram's clothes were not destined for the new breed of Peacocks either; their inbuilt good taste was a little too middle-class. But his skills did give Ingram the opportunity to expand his empire to 15 shops, one cosily sited in Savile Row, as well as create an export business and a flourishing international design consultancy. His King's Road shop paved the way for other small quality boutiques, such as Just Men and Squire, which caught the mood and set up nearby. Not only did he provide the newcomers with potential clients looking for similar items at a lower price, but his shop also served as an excellent visual example of how to dress a shop's interior and how to present the clothes. Carnaby Street's apparent dictum of anything goes was not for Ingram.

Opposite Desmond FitzGerald, Knight of Glin, understatedly elegant in pale beige single-breasted gabardine suit with lilac shirt and tie. *Vogue*, 15 March 1969. Photograph: Patrick Lichfield.

Above In town Jocelyn Stevens, editor-in-chief of *Queen* magazine, wore suits from Cooling, Lawrence & Wells, Maddox Street, preferring old clothes for the country. 'I am not a dresser,' he claimed. 'One simply can't wear anything that is in any way unusual without causing a total furore'. *Men in Vogue*, November 1965. Photograph: Ron Traeger.

It was at this moment that the names that would epitomize the changing times were beginning to make their mark. These names would conjure a freer world that offered a man a variety of acceptable ways in which he could please himself and stamp individuality on his appearance if he had the money.

Many of the clothes would be extravagant, cut from colourful fabrics not seen on a man's back in recent history. In addition to velvet suits in a wide range of colours, there would be shirts in pure silks and wide ties in a blaze of hand-blocked patterns, and everything that appeared would be considered both brave and fashionably acceptable because of the socially impeccable sources that supplied them. Wearing clothes that drew attention to the wearer no longer cast a shadow over a man's virility or his sexual inclination although in any case, this being the time of liberation, being gay did not matter. Until then, pink may have been considered a girl's colour, but a fashionable man could now wear a pink shirt, and pink slacks too, if he so wished. Soon, even those men who had changed their appearance least, had changed a lot.

Spotting the trend, manufacturers quickly brought in younger designers to inject life into their products, from knitwear to raincoats. London stores like Austin Reed, Jaeger, Simpsons and Moss Bros opened more fashionable, youthful departments – not always with much success.

Now that appearances mattered, the range of grooming products expanded to match the mood. Branded colognes and moisturizers appeared alongside ranges of after-shaves and deodorants. And to meet the demands of longer hairstyles, a new breed of hairdressing salon appeared.

Enter the Peacock . . .

Opposite Barry Sainsbury, director of Mr Fish, impeccably turned out in summer suit and Mr Fish's distinctive shirt and tie. *The Sunday Times*, 15 June 1969. Photograph: David Montgomery/Fashion Museum, Bath.

THE MODEL AGENCY

English Boy Ltd

KING'S ROAD

In 1953 Jean Scott-Atkinson opened Britain's first agency to represent both male and female models and called it Scotty's. Until then, when a man was required as a prop in a photograph or on the catwalk during a fashion show, friends or out-of-work actors were coerced into making an appearance. Before breaking into movies Roger Moore was on Scotty's books and graced knitting patterns wearing handmade sweaters.

By the 1960s a number of agencies had men on their books, but most of these models professed to be doing the work simply for the money in order to travel the world, build a boat, or buy a beach house in Minorca, rather than as a profession. Being a male model had a louche quality about it, given to homosexual innuendo. Magazine advertisements of the period show the same selection of amorphous, often barely photogenic, men in various forms of dress selling anything from the new Rover to Y-fronts. Often they clutch a pipe, cigar or rolled newspaper in what was perceived as a masculine image, hackneyed though it was even then.

Challenging this image in 1967 was an agency calling itself English Boy, which opened in Chelsea. It offered a new kind of dandy, young skinny men who seemed rarely to smile. These models were all amateurs, of course, and all were familiar faces on the King's Road. English Boy was established by (Sir) Mark Palmer, a 25-year-old Old Etonian and Oxford graduate, who the newspapers continually reminded readers was a page at the coronation of

Queen Elizabeth II. His partners Kelvin Webb and Trisha Locke ran the business from premises above the Quorum boutique in Shawfield Street where designer Ossie Clark was based.

'Our intention was to change the image of British manhood and put a man, as opposed to a woman, on all magazine covers. All male models until then seemed to be big Australians with big chests – we wanted beautiful men,' says Trisha Locke. In April 1967 one of their models, Bill Chenail (33, 26, 33"), was heralded as the male answer to Twiggy and the agency soon gained notoriety by signing up well-known faces about town, both men and women, such as Brian Jones of the Rolling Stones and Christine Keeler fresh from the Profumo scandal.

Overseas newspapers gave English Boy due coverage. The *New York Times* took a humorous slant as did France's *L'Express* when, on 10 April 1967, Patrick Thévenon wrote that 'the squeaky clean era of fashion photography seems to be well over', with the strapping models of the previous era replaced by 'young Englishmen, taciturn, longhaired and well bred who look as though descended from The Princes in the Tower'. 'Of course,' says Locke now, 'we were innocent and didn't really know what to do.' Yet English Boy paved the way for things to come and when Jose Fonseca, who had handled the models' bookings, set up her own agency it instantly became one of the fashion and advertising worlds' great international successes, Models One.

Opposite 'English Manhood 1967' – so claimed the publicity campaign headline accompanying the photograph of models at the launch of the new agency English Boy. At the centre is Mark Palmer who headed the enterprise. 1967. Photograph: Ray Rathbone. Private collection.

Above Promoting a return to a sleek, smooth haircut in a move away from Swinging London's longer hair, Vidal Sassoon selected shoe designer Manolo Blahnik as his distinctive model. Summer 1974.

CHAPTER 3

Enter the Peacock

1965-73

Peacocks dressed proudly. Their aim was to attract attention and favourable comment. And as the 1960s progressed, so too did Peacock style. Rich silks, cashmeres and velvets more usually associated with women's clothes, and frequently costly, were commandeered. Fine furs were appropriated. Peacocks plundered the past and travelled the world to find new ways of dressing. Ethnic fabrics followed in the wake of the hippy trail to India, while antique cloths and lace created romantic heroes in the spirit of Tom Jones. Colour was mixed with colour, pattern was layered upon pattern. All selected with care but then worn lightly. As rules of propriety and gender were broken and men's fashion became ever more acceptable, so did hair styling and male grooming products. And the influence of the Peacock Revolution rippled out from London, its epicentre, throughout Britain to Europe and beyond, nurturing a new generation of designers and regenerating the retail industry as it went.

Like their sartorial predecessors, the Mods and the Teds, emerging Peacocks were clothes-obsessed, albeit in a different way; Peacocks did not come from a London subculture and so did not have to strive to make a mark on the streets. In fact, initially, most of the men who would come visually to symbolize a Peacock had received a textbook privileged upbringing outside London. Most were well-born and ex-public school (major and minor). Some had aristocratic lineage.

Unlike the coterie of much older dandies, epitomized by 'Bunny' Roger (p.32) and Cecil Beaton (p.30), who dressed with lavish self-regard and could still be seen clinging to Mayfair-like social salons, the younger generation of Peacocks did not exclude new members on the basis of class. The background of the new dandies had given them abundant self-confidence and for them race, religion and class were of negligible importance. All were lured to London by the stories of the first sparks of liberation ignited in the late 1950s by earlier sets of upper-class young men and women who had enlivened society. In London work might be found, rents were cheap and fun was to be had. (For fun read sex, parties and late nights.) In London most would be beyond the range of parental control or supervision; their independence could be given reality. This was the spirit of the times.

What made Peacocks stand out was their attitude to personal appearance. They were, above all else, individuals, each one ready to create a new personal self, each one – to use the maxim of the time – doing his own thing. 'It was as if wealthy or aristocratic young people had realized there was a flamboyant world outside their world and were coming out of their shells – though to us already here this life was normal,' recounts designer Peter Golding, recalling the Peacocks' gradual appearance. By 'here' Golding is referring to his own early days immersed in men's fashion, when he was supplying Naval bridge coats to Chelsea's trend-setting John Michael shop in the King's Road,

Opposite Laurence Harvey, actor, unmissable in a generously cut fur coat. Photograph: Ron Traeger.

coats that in true entrepreneurial spirit he was buying retail, off-the-peg, at Moss Bros. Golding would later set up a serious wholesale business, based in Savile Row, which supplied shirts made in India to the numerous boutiques then multiplying on the high street. He also created a jeans range that would become popular in the United States, the home of jeans, and by the mid-1970s – when fashion turned glitzy – his retail foray, a shop called Ace in the King's Road, was pleasing customers like Freddie Mercury, Elton John and Rod Stewart. More Glitter Man than Glam Rock is how Golding describes it.

But where Mods and Teds wore clothes as a means of setting themselves apart from their backgrounds as they identified with a peer group, the Peacocks were not concerned with anyone outside their various immediate circles. For them clothes were simply flamboyant indulgence.

Many worked, often in a dilettante manner, in jobs their fathers had negotiated for them, but a considerable number of this elite were inspired by entrepreneurial spirit and determined to succeed in the arts, fashion or media where others of all social strata were already trail-blazing. To fortify them, some had allowances from Daddy who was praying that, in spite of temptation, his progeny would soon be settling down to career, family life and heirs. Peacock girlfriends often went to socially acceptable secretarial

colleges before being launched into working life, seeking jobs at advertising agencies and fashion magazines or, much less taxing, as assistants to decorators and antique dealers. London's premier auction houses were particularly welcoming.

As a result of their social backgrounds the first wave of this new generation of Peacocks, in the 1960s, were drawn to the finer shops around Bond Street, where clothes may have been expensive but traditional values such as quality were assured. Since childhood they were familiar with the prestigious names of Jermyn Street's shirt-makers and the expertise of Savile Row tailors, where son would follow father into becoming a valued customer. Most knew precisely where you could get specific items: Gucci for loafers, Cartier for the decade's most covetable Tank watch, W. Bill, Scott Adie or N. Peal for Shetland and cashmere sweaters, and Dunhill for a gold-plated lighter engraved with one's initials. Something for the country like a waterproof coat? Well, Cordings in Piccadilly rarely disappointed.

However, although the emerging Peacock may have looked passable as he was, like many of his contemporaries, he secretly wanted clothes that looked different; 'trendy' was the word. Where a father might have refused to say who his tailor was, the theory being that you wore the suit, the suit did not wear you (the answer to the intrusive question 'Whose suit is it?' would be 'Mine'), his

Opposite Julian Ormsby Gore, who worked in film production, adopted more sophisticated Peacock colours: dark green ruffled shirt, to order by Philip Stevens, Soho. *Men in Vogue*, November 1965. Photograph: Ron Traeger.
Above Ossie Clark, fashion designer, in a distinctive snakeskin jacket. Photograph: *Evening Standard*/Getty Images.

Above Rod Stewart, at home in Surrey, in striped bolero jacket fastened by silver clasps worn over chiffon shirt with yellow satin trousers and trailing scarf. Most of his clothes were made by Marisa Martin, 146 Brompton Road, Knightsbridge. *Evening Standard*, 12 September 1973. Photograph: Roy Jones/*Evening Standard*/Getty Images.

son was only too proud to say where he had bought his. So, as new shops opened, loyalties changed, often coaxed by girlfriends or sisters determined to be seen with a man keeping up with the times. As Peacocks wanted to be – and generally were – unashamedly admired by women, they were not afraid of fashion. Or of being considered fashionable. Or of admiring the clothes worn by other Peacocks.

It is often suggested that this move towards flamboyance was primarily gay-driven (though 'queer' or 'homosexual' were the two words in currency in the 1960s). Whether there were a considerable number of gay Teds is a matter of conjecture; certainly Mods, with their fastidious attention to fashion's changes, were always taunted as gay even if they were not. But, then as now, although there were gay, snappy dressers and shop staff were predominantly and unmistakably gay, the over-whelming percentage of Peacock men wearing the new colourful finery were unquestionably heterosexual. Like the strutting peacock with his eye-catching tail plumage, this extravagance was a way of signalling presence and availability to the opposite sex.

Rupert Lycett Green believed that the men who dressed at his shop Blades chose clothes 'to pull the birds', and Erica Crome, a fashion editor whose career took her from *Menswear*, the trade publication, through to *Queen*, *Harpers & Queen*, *Vogue* and even top-shelf magazine *Mayfair*, where her pages 'had the only people

with clothes on', agrees with the theory, though seeing it from a woman's point of view:

The look was very much London based, but these Sixties men were able to look flamboyant – as if saying look at me. Girls loved it; it was pulling power.

One of the bench marks of the period was the fact that for the first time men could be sex objects. Until then only women had been considered this way. The liberation of the female body through the contraceptive pill in turn liberated the male body through clothes.

For the first time men's bottoms looked sexy. Until then – just look at pictures of men in the 1940s and 1950s – men's trousers rarely fitted over the seat; they were baggy.

By 1965 the number of Peacocks had increased to such a degree that November 1965 *Men in Vogue* reported on the fact. In a group, the magazine stated, Peacocks always seemed to attract attention by their resplendent appearance; individually they may have been startling but together they formed a flamboyant collage in which not a single detail of one was out of step with another. 'Peacocks,' the magazine added, 'all have the same taste, but a taste so wide that they could never at the same time look the same'.

This was, of course, a reflection of 1960s-perceived good taste. Seen

Above The Rolling Stones free concert in Hyde Park, 5 July 1969. Mick Jagger wore a 'dress' designed by Michael Fish. Photograph: MirrorPix.

from the twenty-first century, much might be considered theatrical. But as the mood of the decade was to dress up and have fun, good taste had little true relevance. Good taste was in the eye of the beholder. Clothes needed to be eye-catching. Nothing else mattered.

In spite of this apparent dedication to the cause, the aim of the day was not sartorial perfection but insouciant style. A Peacock dressed with confidence to please himself, teaming his clothes accordingly with instinctive easy-going care. You might not have admired the way he mixed his colours or patterns, but that was personal opinion; a Peacock always took trouble putting his clothes together. Then he wore them with nonchalance. Summing up the mood in 1968, couturier Hardy Amies, a confirmed Peacock himself, wrote in his *ABC of Men's Fashion*: 'A man should look as if he had bought his clothes with intelligence, put them on with care and then forgotten all about them'.

Many of the new shops that now targetted Peacocks were owned or financially backed by people whose names and photographs graced the pages of Society magazines, especially at weddings and Royal race meetings. Being a shopkeeper was, to use the day's terminology, 'a gas' (at this point Clement Freud announced, 'One feels almost a fool if one doesn't own a boutique'). Most of their customers would initially be friends, or friends of friends. London's aspiring new elite, no longer bound by class and with spending money in its pockets, could enter their social sphere later.

The truth was, where you shopped mattered. If a jacket came from Blades (see p.94–103) or Mr Fish (see p.104–17), for instance, then whatever the colour, shape or fabric, it was deemed fashionable. If you wore a pastel suit from Hung on You (see p.90–95), this was a sign that you were liberated. And when Mick Jagger wore what appeared to be a floaty white dress for the Rolling Stones' free concert in Hyde Park (5 July 1969), this was judged acceptable, too. Unconventional his outfit may have been, but if a Rolling Stone wanted to appear in a dress in public that was fine, especially as it was made by Michael Fish, who was renowned for being able to create look-at-me outfits when asked. As designer Ossie Clark once said, a girl can walk down the King's Road dressed in two banana skins, but they must be well-designed banana skins. The same applied to men's clothes.

The important tailoring names to conjure with alongside Blades and Mr Fish were Tom Gilbey (see p.118–25) and Tommy Nutter (see p.128–33). Both were young careerists: Gilbey was a menswear couturier intent on making his mark by changing the way men dressed; Nutter was Savile Row's trendiest tailor, competing with the establishment by injecting a fresh outlook into a staid profession. In a league of his own was Doug Hayward (see p.124–7), an East Ender and tailor by trade and inclination, who had set his sights on competing directly with the old fashioned craftsmen of Savile Row. Setting up club-like premises in Mount Street, just paces from the grand Connaught Hotel, he discreetly

Above Fashionable group: Michael Fish (left), Christopher Lynch (second left) and David Mlinaric (right) at the home of Christopher Gibbs. Photograph: Terrence Spencer/Time Life Pictures/Getty Images, 1966.

Overleaf, pages 76–77 Style arbiters Julian Ormsby Gore, Christopher Gibbs, Nicholas Gormanston, Jane Ormsby Gore and Victoria Ormsby Gore (left to right). What they wore set the pace. Photograph: Ron Traeger, 1965.

suited and became a lasting friend of a wide circle of the day's Peacocks, including rising-star actors like Michael Caine, Terence Stamp and Roger Moore.

Taking the fashion-minded revolution to even more dilettante extremes were two shops in an esoteric world of their own making. Like their contemporaries, the entrepreneurs behind Granny Takes a Trip (see p.84–9) and Hung on You came from upper-class backgrounds; unlike their contemporaries, who had set up shop around Bond Street, they chose unconventional Chelsea. Their idiosyncratic shops, with more than just a touch of dandy exuberance and amateurishness about them, made both the proprietors and the clothes instantly distinctive. Both boutiques seemed to aspire to rare, hippie-inspired creativity – the hippieness coming as much from the mingling scents of marijuana, patchouli and incense that charged the air as the clothes themselves which, mostly, had a picturesque romanticism about them. When these two shops first opened, visitors got the impression that the owners just wanted somewhere to make enough money to support them as they entertained friends, smoked a little dope and enjoyed dressing up. But both places had a talent for introducing clothes that created an instantly exclusive image and customer numbers quickly swelled as pop groups with their hangers-on, fleeing Carnaby Street, crowded in after the Beatles and the Rolling Stones took to shopping there.

Taking the grand stance *Queen* magazine (November 1965) reflected the belief that 'British remains best': 'No longer are men forced to get shirts from Bloomingdales, shoes from Rome, and suits run up in twelve-and-a-half minutes by little men in Hong Kong … Chrome plated Modness is dead – [it] can be left to architectural students or to pop groups with a name to make.' With customary manicured prose *Queen* continued with the advice that 'Something more personalized is the present aim. Those in the know remain loyal to John Michael, the Savile Row of the Carnaby Street look. And the posher ones [referring to their own readers, presumably] go to Blades – the Carnaby Street of the Savile Row look'.

It was this good-tempered, cool attitude that gave men's fashion its new-found legitimacy and would prove a lasting influence on the clothing industry. With the seeds sown originally by the Mods, followed by the upmarket acceptance of dandyism, men's fashion had turned into an honourable, commercial proposition. Shops selling dull men's merchandise across Britain began to disappear, or rapidly changed their image along with the merchandise they stocked. What was available in London would soon be available everywhere.

It might seem odd, many decades later, when all major international labels take on a trained designer to revamp and reposition their products in the market place, that when clothes

Opposite Mark Palmer, romantically languid in soft double-breasted velvet suit, cotton shirt and silk tie. This was 1965 casual formality. Photograph: Ron Traeger, 1965.
Above James Fox dressed by Mr Fish for Robert Parrish's 1968 film *Duffy*. He wears a dinner jacket in domino-patterned stripes with ruffled shirt and velvet bow tie. Photograph: Fashion Museum, Bath.

Above For the premiere of *Duffy* James Fox echoed his screen image with the frilled shirt from Mr Fish that helped to create the Peacock look. *Daily Express*, 25 January 1968. Photograph: Larry Ellis/*Daily Express*/Hulton Archive/Getty Images.

manufacturers did so in the 1960s, it was as if a retailing revolution was taking place. Manufacturers rushed to employ young designers to inject life into product ranges, from knitwear to raincoats, in order to tap into the flow of money being lavished on clothes by an apparently insatiable new generation. London stores like Austin Reed, Jaeger, Moss Bros and Simpsons, aiming to capture attention, took on young buyers to open departments that would offer irresistible temptation. In the hope of meeting these demands, many of the dowdiest shops took the plunge, too, often putting outrageously designed clothes of dubious taste, colour and style into their windows. For them, the times were desperate.

Austin Reed had seen the need to respond to changes in the way upscale shops were dressing fashion-conscious Peacocks and looked at the opportunities presented by the Carnaby Street explosion. They appointed Colin Woodhead, who joined the store from *Town* magazine, where he was fashion editor. His role at Austin Reed was to create Cue, a trend boutique for the store's chain of shops. 'It was an exciting time to be in retail. It was like cutting a path through a jungle, no one had done it before,' says Woodhead now. 'I had always dressed differently,' he adds, and indeed he had. For a debutante party he wore Albert Finney's frilly shirt from Tom Jones with black stretch trousers and high cavalry boots. 'A great success with the girls,' he says. 'It was about as near to being a dandy as you could get in 1964. But, of course, you had to be more circumspect for work.'

In fact by 1965 there were flared trousers, kipper ties, long highwayman coats, frilly shirts, flowing silk scarves, buckled shoes – and boots that zipped up the calf to the knee had begun to make an appearance as boutiques attempted with some bravado to catch the mood. For Peacocks who understood the art of dressing there were velvet or corduroy suits and velvet dinner jackets, worn in traditional style with evening shirts and large, floppy velvet bow ties. Romantic? Yes, mostly. Elegant, certainly.

A Peacock wanted to look good, well turned-out from head to toe. The scruffy style that came with the advent of jeans, T-shirts and kaftans would not do at all. To wear the clothes properly it helped to be slim, if not skinny, although as these were the days before fast food obesity was relatively unknown and most people were youthfully slim.

Hair was now longer, more natural and better cut. In fact men had already begun to go to women's hairdressers, often after hours, for a decent, styled haircut and possibly some highlighting or colouring. The days of those barbers who offered merely short-back-and-sides and 'something-for-the-weekend-Sir?' were numbered. As men grew their hair, so barbers evolved into hairdressers with salons rather than shops and the selection of contraceptives at pharmacies became more visible on counters.

Respected Establishment barbers, like Truefitt & Hill and Trumpers,

Above Christopher Gibbs, antique dealer, known for the attention he paid to detail, especially in clothes, wears a green drill jacket from Blades, handmade shirt by Philip Stevens and silk tie from Top Gear. *Men in Vogue*, November 1965. Photograph: Ron Traeger.

as well as those at leading department stores, began to change staff in order to keep up, while big name salons, like Vidal Sassoon, made a concerted effort to tap the male market. Opening the first groovy salons dedicated to men were Gary Craze at Sweenys in Beauchamp Place and Keith at Scissors at the World's End, Chelsea, while the exclusive Peter Smith only took clients privately and on personal recommendation at changing addresses known only to the select few. All were successful. Trying to add his own macho touch was Simon Boyle, a partner in a wig-making company and front man at King's Road tailors Allsopp, Brindle and Boyle. He launched false Viva Zapata moustaches made from real hair at £2 each. This absurdity saw publicity in tabloid newspapers and then disappeared.

In *Men in Vogue* (November 1966) Angus McGill wrote about the way men's hairstyles were changing:

At this very minute 15,000 gallant barbers selflessly man their posts, clipping and chopping and shearing ... At one time all these barbers did much the same job. Some charged more than others but it was still the same basic ten minutes under the scissors and clippers wherever you went. But today this ancient profession is riven down the middle. One the one hand there are old style barbers clipping away as ever they did. On the other are the new men, barbers who don't even call themselves barbers any more. They call themselves hair stylists and do things to a man's head

that would have been unthinkable in our father's day. They wave, they shape, they tint ... with such success that in the past five years the appearance of an Englishman has been subtly but noticeably changed. He looks younger, sharper, altogether more kempt. He's just got a better haircut, that's all.

Changing male hairstyles elicited comment from men and women alike. Long hair, it appeared, caused outrage among some, its length symbolizing decadence or, at the very least, effeminacy. And when colognes, moisturizers and, great heavens, make-up were introduced, many were speechless. The 1960s running joke claimed that make-up appealed to gay men who, like women, lived in a neurosis-filled world of having to appeal to men.

Men's make-up at this time was little more than aftershaves or fake-tan creams that hopefully would enhance the face rather than turn it orange – and for the adventurous perhaps moisturizer. But, as Michael Caine said in interview on this subject, 'Men are not meant to look pretty'.

However, Mary Quant tested the water by introducing a Make-up Box for Men, while on the third floor of Barbara Hulanicki's Biba, in the men's department, there were elegant black marble and walnut veneer display cabinets proffering Biba's Men's Health cosmetic range that included a moisturizer and a lime-scented skin freshener. In South Molton Street, Glints bravely opened to

Above The new elegant formality: three-piece purple velvet evening suit teamed with chiffon shirt, by Thea Porter. 1972. Private collection.

Above Peter Hinwood, antique dealer and prototype Rocky in the *Rocky Horror Show*, in black and white cashmere sports jacket, £95, with striped silk tie and spotted handkerchief from Sulka. *Evening Standard*, 18 December 1974. Photograph: Manolo Blahnik.

Above Miguel Bose, musician and actor (left) and Patrice Calmettes, photographer, theatrically dressed in ethnic fabrics. Calmettes' coat is made from Benares scarves of beaten silver studs. At Essences, King's Road. *Evening Standard*, 5 December 1973. Photograph: Anthony Crickmay. V&A Archive.

Opposite Miguel Bose and Patrice Calmettes in black velvet jackets, white shirts, black trousers, chains and sash. All from Essences, King's Road. *Evening Standard*, 5 December 1973. Photograph: Anthony Crickmay. V&A Archive.

offer men total grooming treatments that included facials and eyebrow contouring.

Make-up in terms of powder-and-paint was never a reality but aftershaves like Old Spice, Imperial Leather and Pino Silvestre were superseded by more expensive colognes from Jermyn Street's Floris or Guerlain (Vetiver, Habit Rouge) or Dior (Eau Sauvage). The products that men now began to seek out were more than simply a choice of hair dressings or deodorants. Gradually the first selections of face scrubs and eye-bag creams appeared. From New York in 1965 came Estée Lauder's all-encompassing grooming aids under the banner of Aramis. Men's grooming, like men's fashion, had moved to another plateau of acceptance.

While Peacocks continued to live their exclusive lives, mainstream men's fashion, kick-started by the appearance of the Mods and the extraordinary fame and influence of Carnaby Street, was gathering momentum. The comatose years of Britain's fashion manufacturing and retailing sector were over, just as they were in Europe and the United States, where young people and new-found wealth were having a similar galvanizing effect on the marketplace.

In Paris, Pierre Cardin and Ted Lapidus were making successful commercial inroads into menswear retailing, changing pre-conceived ideas of a man's suit and its silhouette. It was Cardin, for example, who first showed the collarless jackets that would be the Beatles' distinctive uniform in the early years of their incarnation (see Dougie Millings, pp.46–7) and for many years his fashion shows were greeted as divine revelation by French fashion journalists and covered in depth in French newspapers and on television. Although also inspired by the Space Age, it was Cardin's tailored suits, with their youthful cut (tight-fitting jackets nipped in at the waist and deep vents at the back), which were seen to breath new life into staid traditions. (His recommendation that the trousers be tucked into knee-length boots, however, did not appeal much to men in France, or in Britain.) His steadily increasing fame and influence led the chain of multiple tailors, Neville Reed and John Temple, to sign a contract with him. Their intention was to introduce Cardin's designs to British men and so meet the perceived competition that would be generated by the home-grown Hardy Amies' association with the Hepworths chain. Cardin's suits to measure cost around £20, as did those with the Amies label. As it happened neither Cardin nor Amies would make an appreciable impression on the way British men dressed – their designs appeared to have prissy surplus detailing rather than a new direction. However, Cardin went on to international consultancy, creating a recognized brand in more spheres than just clothes, and Amies' trunk shows (static presentations of his collections) in the Far East earned him welcome recognition.

Also in Paris but smartly upmarket, on a corner of the Place de la Madeleine, was the store of Nino Cerruti, an Italian with manufacturing interests. His clothes could be found in upscale London boutiques like Piero de Monzi in Fulham Road, alongside the trendy San Frediano restaurant, and later in a shop bearing the Cerruti name in Bond Street. On opening in Paris in 1964, he brought in a talented young Italian designer, who had been working at Hitman, Cerruti's clothing manufacturing company. Known simply as Giorgio, his role was to create the menswear line. Like Cardin, Valentino and Yves Saint Laurent, Giorgio often visited London, taking inspiration from street fashion as well as from the city's more traditional gentlemen's outfitters. When he established himself in Milan ten years later to introduce his own menswear collection, he used his own name, Giorgio Armani. A year later he introduced his first womenswear collection. For him, as the adage goes, the rest was history.

In autumn 1965 it was the turn of the United States to clothe the British man. Austin Reed had launched its new division, aimed at customers aged between 25 and 35, with the intention of providing fashionable clothes made to the high standards expected of the store rather than those of neighbouring Carnaby Street. 'The Austin Reed suppliers were wonderful,' says Colin Woodhead, 'and they adapted quickly to fashion ideas knowing that Carnaby Street was unstoppable. But we needed to respond to the imminent arrival of foreign designers like Pierre Cardin who were looking to expand

into Britain. So we introduced New York designer John Weitz, a sportswear designer famed for his casual clothes.' In conversation Woodhead continues, 'It was the pull of America. We couldn't move into jeans and denim, but as Weitz designs were fresh, using great colour and fabrics, they would be a great antidote to Cardin and Ted Lapidus'. As he had challengingly explained in an interview with America's influential *Daily News Record* in May 1966: 'People want comfort first and looks second. I am certain Cardin is going in the wrong direction for the United States and Britain where we've broken down the rigid way of life. Young people don't stand around like cardboard dummys [sic]. Cardin may have an effect on the shape of coats but ...' The implication was: nothing more.

As the 1970s progressed and contracts expired, the foreign names quietly disappeared, not into oblivion but back home or into less publicized arenas. It would be some time before names like Giorgio Armani, Ralph Lauren and Dolce & Gabbana would enter the void.

Above Yves Saint Laurent in London in a sand-coloured cotton, safari-inspired, shirt that was part of a collection that gave his distinctive image to the Rive Gauche shops. 10 September 1969. Photograph: Bentley Archive/Popperfoto/Getty Images.

Above Tuty Franco Da Sa in Nino Cerruti's distinctive blouson jacket, still sharply tailored but more casual in style, 28 February 1973. Private collection.

THE WORLD'S END

JOHN PEARSE AND NIGEL WAYMOUTH

Granny Takes a Trip

KING'S ROAD

One of the key places where pop stars and toffs socialized, and often shopped, was Granny Takes a Trip, a boutique of an unclassified species that opened in December 1965 at 488 King's Road, on a dilapidated stretch awaiting gentrification known to all as the World's End, after a pub of that name that had serviced the locals since Victorian times. In fashion terms this outpost was in unknown territory, about as far from the trendy boutiques around Sloane Square as it was possible to go. Diagonally across the road were an ailing Woolworth's store, another weary pub, a greengrocer and a housing estate. The shop's immediate neighbour was a sedate office of the Royal British Legion, the Poppy Day charity that provides help to the serving and ex-service members of the Army, Navy and Air Force and their families. Rents here were low – for Granny's three storeys it was £14 a week – but with a graphic façade that dramatically lit up the paint-peeling terraced houses round about, the shop developed a regular clientele within weeks of opening.

The shop's image was eclectic; as hippie as it was Mod, as dandy as it was Peacock. Its name was deliberately anti-Establishment and while 'Takes a Trip' was an obvious reference to LSD, the recreational drug of the day, the owners insisted that the reference was meant to be amusing, the suggestion being that when dear Granny sees familiar Victoriana being worn by young people, she is transported pleasurably back to her youth. Naturally, given the alleged free-wheeling lifestyle that revolved around

the shop and its owners, little credence was given to this explanation. For a long time the rumour persisted that the labels of Granny garments were impregnated with LSD and should therefore be licked.

The shop was the brainchild of Nigel Waymouth (famed then for his Afro hairstyle and gold-framed granny spectacles rather than for his graphic design and the posters that so encapsulated the period) and his girlfriend Sheila Cohen. Also known for a while as the actress Sheila Troy, she was an obsessive collector of vintage clothes, which she purchased mostly at Portobello market and jumble sales. She had amassed such a vast collection that, at Waymouth's insistence, she was now prepared to sell. Attractive period clothes had become a must-have alternative fashion and were much sought after.

Joining them in the shop was John Pearse, a distinctively dressed Mod in his fledgling years as well as a former Savile Row apprentice tailor, who had polished his skills during three years with Hawes & Curtis. He had an extraordinarily sharp, visual, possibly unique way of dressing and his appearance was unlike that of anyone else at the time. His role was to adapt vintage clothes according to 1960s trends and bring his tailoring experience to the enterprise by introducing his own designs. So while Cohen sold her feather boas and her Victorian, 1920s and 1930s dresses to women, Pearse created the men's clothes.

Opposite John Pearse with Regine Boulanger outside the World's End pub, King's Road, in 1966. Both, of course, are dressed in Granny's finery. Pearse believed 'the modern dandy need not be rich to be fashionable'. Photograph: Colin Maher.

Above A Nigel Waymouth poster for Granny Takes a Trip. The caption reads 'Buy Granny Takes a Trip and join the Brain-Drain!'.

As the vintage stock sold, so Cohen introduced velvet skirts and lace trimmed blouses while Pearse, using teams of talented outworkers whom he had encountered in earlier years, took his imaginative ideas further, creating the clothes that Granny's would come to be known for: suits, jackets and trousers in surprising fabrics, colours and floral prints. Teamed with these were equally eye-catching shirts in extravagant materials. Granny's philosophy reflected Oscar Wilde's maxim: 'One should either be a work of art, or wear a work of art'.

The shop's appeal was pitched exclusively at a social strata with money – particulary at emerging pop groups, music being the trio's abiding passion. So the first customers included, alongside budding Peacocks, those ubiquitous shoppers the Beatles, the Who and the Rolling Stones, who were themselves rapidly turning into the works of art of the period. The Beatles wore Granny's clothes on the cover of their album *Revolver* (1966), as did the Rolling Stones on *Between the Buttons* (1967).

'Granny's was the zeitgeist of the times,' says Waymouth in conversation in June 2009. 'It was Mod-ish, art school, and yet upmarket. I was the product of a grammar school and the London School of Economics, not public school like the people in West End boutiques like Blades, while Pearse was an ex-Mod. But we mixed easily with the young Chelsea Set and fitted in. It was the spirit of the times – everyone mixed.'

Much to the pleasure of the neighbourhood and the passengers on the passing No.11 and No.22 buses, the façade of the shop changed according to whim and was an expression of Waymouth's growing interest in graphics. For the shop's opening its frontage was painted dramatically with vivid red Art Nouveau lettering on a jet-black background, but within months the plate glass window would be obscured completely by new artwork. The graphic image of the Red Indian chief Running Bear was followed in 1967 by the face of a 1930s showgirl depicted Pop Art style, the slender gap between her pouting lips giving a tantalizing view of the shop's interior. In 1968, to much consternation and amusement, the front half of a 1948 Dodge car was bolted to the window to look as though it had shot through the glass pane and was heading across the shop's forecourt onto the pavement. No one had seen anything like it. (The local Council would ultimately order its removal on the grounds that it was a dangerous hazard.)

Due to its more art school than retail presentation, Granny's looked knowingly mysterious and forbidding. Inside, its purple walls were decorated with Aubrey Beardsley's erotic prints and the dark interior was heavy with the scent of incense, seemingly chosen to mask the heady fumes of what was then legally-termed 'a banned substance', which appeared to echo the message in the shop's name. To the uninitiated the whole effect was arrogantly intimidating. It proclaimed: 'If you don't belong, don't enter.'

Above While the short stretch of the King's Road known as the World's End was still ungentrified, Granny Takes a Trip with its changing façade stood out, becoming one of Chelsea's landmarks. In 1967 it took on the image of a 1930s Hollywood showgirl. Photograph: David Graves/Rex Features.

In reality the clothes were gentle, a fanciful mixture of camp, whimsy, Victoriana, beatnik and drawing-room dandy. The shop was excitedly catering for an exclusive in-crowd, one that wanted to dress-up, to be noticed. A typical Granny's male customer was expected to dress with a touch of flamboyance.

'Our first clients were what were loosely called at that time the Chelsea Set,' recalls Pearse. 'The average man in the street was dreary, but our clientele was not. Not at all.'

The vintage garments sold well. While many were cannibalized and adapted by Pearse to be made into other garments, they also had to manufacture their own ranges to match demand.

We had to do something,' says Pearse. 'So Mrs Trott in New Cross came back into my life to make shirts. For some reason there were a lot of shirtmakers in New Cross and I knew her in my Mod youth when she made some for me. Of course, now no expense was spared; we bought beautiful floral and Liberty print fabrics at retail prices at Liberty's department store in Regent Street. I had this idea for a long, floppy rounded collar, shaped like a three-penny piece. We had six made and within minutes of being in the shop, the first one sold.

With Pearse in charge there was an emphasis on tailoring. There were changing selections of soft velvet suits in a variety of colours including pale blue and green. Suits were form-fitting, buttoning tight, with slender arms and generous lapels. Then there were shiny, tightly-fitting, low-slung satin and brocade trousers, and double-breasted jackets tailored in heavy cotton, floral-printed fabrics more usually used for curtains. There were also numerous a variety of amusing ties, many of them with hand-painted kitsch designs. As the front of most shirts appeared to be edged with lacy frills, the ties were mostly bought as presents. There was no doubting, however, that the clothes were gorgeously flamboyant, proclaiming *fin de siècle* dandyism at its finest.

Pearse explains: 'I suppose there was a languid elegance and the clothes did look decadent. It was a sort of Art Nouveau decadence. The Granny look was tailored and fitted, with exotic, ruffled, tight shirts that harked back to Baudelaire and Oscar Wilde. As we got going our life and world was simply Granny's and the King's Road. In those days you could drive and park anywhere you wanted to in Chelsea. Life went at a leisurely pace. There was nothing digital, only a telephone. No mobile phones, no computers and very little bureaucracy.

'Dare I say it, without sounding too pretentious, it was really the time of the last salons, where you would sit with friends in beautiful houses, in a beautiful room, simply discoursing and smoking, listening to music. There was an ambience; it was so relaxed sometimes you'd drop off to sleep. No one drank much, maybe a

vodka and orange or a scotch and coke; drinks seemed to be sweet then. But certainly no beer, and no jeans; it seemed so very sophisticated. Later you might play roulette or black jack. In those days I'd never been to Notting Hill Gate.

By the day's standards the clothes were considered costly. Shirts sold for 4 to 10 guineas depending on fabric; the floral jackets and those in William Morris patterns sold at a remarkable 15 guineas each. The popular range of skinny velvet, satin and brocade trousers that showed a man's silhouette were 6 guineas. Satin ties were £1 10s.

In fact, it was the range of soft velvet trousers that was an immediate success even though, as they had such narrow legs, the seams on the thighs or the seat often split as men sat down. Not that the wearers seemed to mind; this proved the trousers' authenticity. Their clothes had 'a jaunty elegance that was one step away from destitution,' says Pearse, with the humour of hindsight. 'But no one ever complained.'

However, as Waymouth points out defensively, the clothes were still good quality and made in London's ragtrade area using the same outworkers used by Savile Row tailors. 'People' lived in their trousers day and night,' he explains. 'If you are aged 20 and have paid 10 guineas for a pair of trousers, you're never going to be out of them.'

Granny's only true competition as such was Hung on You, a short distance away. 'They weren't so much competition as brethren. If you couldn't get it there, you came to us. Or vice versa,' says Pearse. 'They did some very original things and Michael Rainey was both charming and clever. I liked his Chairman Mao stuff, but what about his Hobbit gear? I never bought into quaint hobbits.'

At their peak Waymouth claimed: 'We will always do well because people know they can come in here and buy something that no one else has.' And Pearse recalls: 'Granny's was a destination. You knew when American tourists were in town … they all came here. So did people like Brigitte Bardot. It was all good fun. People came to us. We made a lot of money – and spent a lot.'

But like many of the smaller commercial enterprises in the 1960s, its life was limited. There was competition from the new boutiques opening along the King's Road, some of them blatantly copying items that had been Granny's own birthright.

'Initially we made money. Perhaps we were an alternative culture. We didn't want austerity, we didn't want drab, we didn't want to dress in grey. We wanted to put colour on the streets,' says Waymouth.

'The bubble finally burst in the 1970s,' says Pearse. 'There had

been student riots in Paris, race riots in the United States, the Vietnam War – we were aware of it all. Then there was recession. You couldn't leave Britain with more than £50 either. But it was when I went to a shirt-maker off Hoxton Square to collect the dozen shirts I had had made for us, and saw that the shirt-maker had copied them by the hundreds because a buyer in a large retail store had seen them in the workroom and wanted them, I realized we were artsy, not capitalist.'

Pearse adds: 'Granny's had run its course for me by the time we imploded. We were into too many things. Something had to give. We were involved in music – we had a rock 'n' roll band – and Nigel had his poster company producing a huge body of work. I quit, saying I'll take the band, you keep the shop. And when the band quickly imploded too, I went to Rome to work on movies.'

In fact Waymouth's involvement in graphics, working with designer Michael English and as Hapsash and the Coloured Coat, resulted in lasting, iconic, mid-1960s images. Their psychedelic designs appeared on posters and album covers, and many of the original graphic designs, like some of Granny's clothes, are now in the permanent collection of the Victoria and Albert Museum.

With Pearse gone and Waymouth more involved elsewhere, Cohen strived to keep Granny's open and to maintain its original spirit but found the task arduous without her former partners. By

late 1969 two New Yorkers had taken over and with what appeared to be a rhinestone persona that appealed to rock stars, it remained open until 1973. When the shop closed the premises became a greengrocer.

After an extensive period in Italy, Pearse returned to his Savile Row skills setting himself up as an exclusive tailor in a fine Georgian town house in Meard Street, Soho, designing and creating clothes for well-heeled men. But, as he reminisces, 'People always hark back to the 1960s, dipping in as if it was the most exciting time for centuries and I think, in retrospect, for us it really was. Living in a gilded cage, we were blessed. Obviously there were some tragic cases in the 1960s, but for us they were truly great times.'

Waymouth, who evolved into a successful artist and portrait painter, adds: 'The bouillabaisse of the 1960s was a crucible that created lasting change. Everyone mixed and, without trying to sound political, it is that 1960s attitude that has lasted over the decades. You could say everyone is middle-class now.'

Above Granny's constantly reinvented itself: in 1966 with a larger-than-life portrait of Chief Running Bear (right) and in 1968 with the front half of an American Dodge automatic. Photographs: Topfoto.

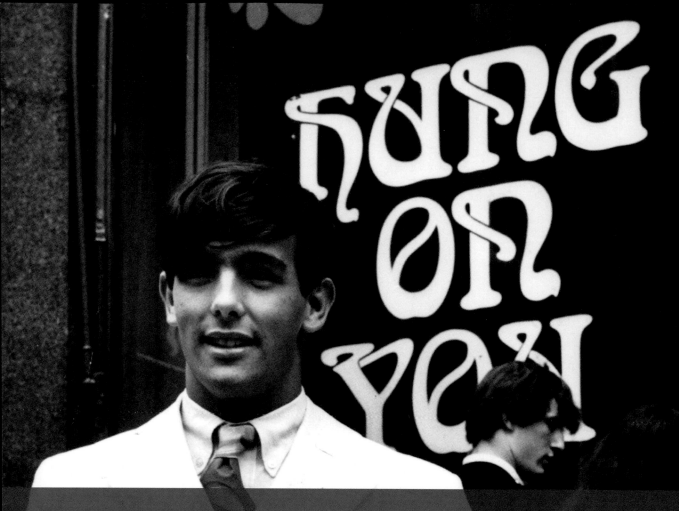

MICHAEL RAINEY

Hung on You

KING'S ROAD

When Hung on You opened in Cale Street, a quiet backwater off the King's Road, in 1965, word spread that it was the most exciting boutique in Chelsea, if not London. It was not, however, for the easily intimidated or anyone unfamiliar with its smart owners, a gilded couple with impeccable connections. With its window painted to resemble Camelot, the shop's aura appeared to proclaim that its hallowed recesses were designated for a select clientele drawn exclusively from the liberated, beautiful people of the day, who were given to reading Tolkien while dressed in velvet jackets and smoking Gitanes – or something more mind-expanding.

Owned by Michael Rainey, who was unmistakably a Peacock in his own right, Hung on You had all the instant trappings of success. Rainey with his enviable appearance, was ideal for heading a shop selling fashionable clothes to men. Tall, good-looking and charming, he had an innate sense of languid style and when in 1966 he married Jane Ormsby Gore, a daughter of Lord Harlech and also a contributing editor on *Vogue*, they made an impressively eye- catching aristocratic couple, seen at the finest places.

Rainey dressed conventionally in well-cut suits that were made for him by tailors in the East End. Not only did they fit impeccably, they also stood out because of the fabrics and the colours he chose. In the days when men customarily wore grey, navy or charcoal, he wore colours more often associated with Sicilian ice cream. Jane Ormsby Gore, his perfect foil, dressed

more dramatically, creating a highly romantic aura with dark colours, velvets, ruffles and decorative accessories seemingly found in the East.

Jonathan Aitken, drawn by the enthusiasm being generated, paid the shop a visit and echoed the views of others on first setting foot there. He described it in *The Young Meteors* (1967) as 'the strangest of young men's fashion establishments in London. The op art designs of the shop front are worthy of a dipsomaniac's nightmare, a positive disincentive to purchase clothes one might think but, in fact, this does not matter much, since for all the apparently alluring decor and brightly-painted shelves, there was not, when I visited it, one single garment visibly on sale in the shop front, nor any sign of an assistant.

This unusual merchandise technique might deter the faint hearted but those who stand their ground long enough will, in time, notice a small hole in the corner of the shop floor with steep precarious steps leading from it to unknown nether regions.

Here he found two assistants, the young man wearing 'a lace shirt and orange jeans too tight for him to move without appearing to be suffering from arthritis' and the girl in 'a miniskirt so short it would not have afforded decent coverage over a pigmy's buttocks, and this was topped by a transparent smock through which it was easy to see she was wearing no other garment of any sort. I felt I

Opposite Neatly tailored, slim, double-breasted suits and jackets that came in a range of pastel colours were part of Hung on You's classic image. This suit, in white, teamed with pale pink shirt and brightly patterned Kipper tie. 1966. Photograph Evening Standard/Getty Images.

Above A Hung on You poster designed in the distinctively psychedelic spirit of the times by Nigel Waymouth and Michael English, the graphic powerhouse duo that comprised Hapsash and the Coloured Coat. Waymouth was also founder of rival King's Road boutique, Granny Takes a Trip.

might be beginning to appreciate the subtleties of Hung on You's sales techniques.'

But for all Aitken's cynical humour, Rainey had a good eye for design and as he told me on hearing Aitken's critique, 'It was a success almost from the day it opened, and when the Who and the Beatles came in, we were made.' Rainey opened the shop without first having trodden the usual fashion designer route of completing a course at art school, or working in fashion retail, in order to understand the industry's problems.

'Basically the design ideas just grew in me, inspired by the people around,' he says, looking back at the heady days of the mid-1960s. 'Like Jane's brother Julian Ormsby Gore, who was a very sharp dresser, and Pete Townshend of the Who. To whatever Townsend wore he gave style – and it looked good in his Lincoln Continental. Then there were men like Marcello Mastroiani in *La dolce vita* and the jazz musicians of the Fifties, all of them with great style, never over-dressing, never gilding the lily, never calling attention to themselves. I really wanted men to look good in more colourful clothes without being swamped by vanity. I suppose I invented the flowered shirt at that time but I really imagined it as inoffensive, not what it would become when it was copied.'

There were sharkskin suits in muted shades of pale pink and pistacchio. There were Byronic shirts in cottons and silks and, as this clique were unlikely to wear jeans, velvet and cotton trousers in a range of colours. To ring the changes, some jackets had velvet cuffs of the same colour, so as to be almost invisible.

'There was no doubt that the shop in Cale Street was successful. It had cachet,' says Jane Rainey wife of Michael and an interior decorator of note, in conversation four decades later. 'There was no mistaking how smart many of the clothes were: jackets that fitted beautifully and had wonderful linings, for example, and were made by wonderful cutters who were properly trained.'

But successful or not, a year later, in the pursuit of true commercial reward, Rainey moved Hung on You to 430 King's Road, a short distance from Granny Takes a Trip. The customers he courted were the Chelsea Set and the King's Road habitués and fashion followers, rather than the smart shoppers of Knightsbridge or Bond Street. This time the shop window was stunningly painted in Art Nouveau style, the work of Tony Little who would later establish Osborne & Little, the renowned fabric suppliers. Inside it was hectically coloured but the clothes remained unusual as well as elegant and romantic, and were still made by traditional tailors and seamstresses in London's East End. Compared to Granny Takes a Trip, Hung on You was more like Blades in its approach to tailoring, while Granny's was more hippie-like, its image, as one Hung on You customer reported, one of Afghan coats and flares.

Above For a *Life* magazine cover, 11 July 1966, a selection of Chelsea's finest were gathered for a photograph in front of a blow-up of Tony Little's design for the Hung On You shop (Ossie Clark is second left). Photograph: Terrence Spencer/Time Life Pictures/Getty Images.

Rainey had a good eye for vintage clothes and, like neighbouring Granny's, he would rework those he liked. Military bandsmen's jackets, guardsmen's trousers and even 1940s demob suits were all restyled. But specially made for the shop were shirts in Liberty prints, shirts with frills, silk shirts, ties, wide leather belts with silver buckles and hand-embroidered jackets. Fine boots and slippers were made from kilims brought back from trips to India, members of this select group being familiar with the ashram trail.

'In retrospect the move to the King's Road was a mistake,' says Jane Rainey in 2009. 'It is a mistake to jump before you have good financial foundations, and we didn't. It took a lot of expenditure: the move, the shop itself, the fittings. Then one of our competitors took our tailors, presumably by offering them more money. It seemed as if there was no question of us ever understanding shop-keeping.'

Michael Rainey explains: 'Everything was new when we started. The dust of Victorian morality, hypocrisy and general stodginess was shaken off. All of a sudden, it was a young world. People started dressing as they wanted to. I brought out flowered shirts and velvet trousers and suits the colour of Smarties.

Clothing was just the wardrobe to go with this exciting world. Everyone we met was infected by the whole atmosphere and the new direction, with its easy-going lifestyles and greater sense of the quality of life. England seemed the most tolerant place on earth except when John Lennon painted his long-wheeled Rolls Royce like a gypsy caravan and angered the old guard.

But then, when we were in the King's Road, we noticed other changes; people were on heroin or cocaine and we saw the pattern of our new order starting to fall apart. Youth was suddenly making a dash for the dosh. We were back where we came in. For us the period was over.

Hung on You closed its doors in September 1968, but during its brief life it was focal to the London fashion scene. When it opened in Cale Street the few clothes on the racks were described by one visitor as extravagantly absurd, but as Michael Rainey's feel for clothes matched the mood of the time, this viewpoint changed. The shop was smart for its Society connections, knowing in its unusual, possibly daring taste, and in tune with London's Peacocks in the way colour was injected into its suavely expensive tailoring. It was an insider's boutique, a place where men could find something out of the ordinary.

And something out of the ordinary happened to the premises, too, after the Raineys had departed. Malcolm McLaren moved in, accompanied by Vivienne Westwood. Together they created a boutique with an ever-changing name and, as always, the fashion scene moved on.

Above Posing to prove that shopping at Hung on You was as normal as shopping at any Chelsea boutique. Photograph: George Freston/Fox Photos/Getty Images.

RUPERT LYCETT GREEN AND CHARLES HORNBY

Blades

SAVILE ROW

While John Stephen set out to design and supply inexpensive clothes for young Mods in Carnaby Street, heading the brave new upmarket Peacock movement was Rupert Lycett Green with his shop Blades, which had a trail of aristocratic connections and Eton as its Alma Mater. Blades' young owners, Lycett Green and partner Charles Hornby, saw themselves as leading avant-garde bespoke tailors, ready to dress customers from social backgrounds similar to their own: wealthy men in their 20s and 30s with money in their pockets and bounteous career opportunities ahead. Like Blades' owners, these smart men-about-town were rethinking their attitudes to the way they dressed, trying to keep up with trendy girlfriends as well as a peer group that was daily becoming more liberated both in style and behaviour.

The doors of 25 Dover Street opened for business in 1962, with the elegant Rupert Lycett Green, then aged 24, an old Etonian, tall, fair, good-looking, well mannered and well connected, at the helm. Lycett Green recalls a diary page in the *Daily Express*, which reported that the son of Angela, Lady Grimthorpe, was entering trade in Mayfair.

If he appeared a little young to head such an ambitious enterprise in competition with London's revered tailors, perhaps he was. But it was in keeping with the spirit of the times; young people with his background were forging ahead in business ventures, catering for each other. Lycett Green had none of the skills

demanded by professional clothes retailing although he appreciated craftsmanship, having had his own clothes made at Davies & Son in Savile Row, and had a consuming interest in clothes – their design, creation and exquisite tailoring. He was determined to understand its complexities even if he could not do the skilled work himself. As he was also in tune with the trends of the day, he presented the perfect image for such an enterprise.

With partner Hornby to handle the finances and Eric Joy as his cutter – Joy was known for his expertise, gained working for tailor Eric Vincent in Sackville Street, as well as for his forthright views and opinions – Lycett Green was ready for business.

In an early interview he explained his decision to go into tailoring by saying that where once young men of his background would have followed their fathers into the City or into estate management, now they were starting their own insurance companies, their own restaurants or their own nightclubs. The implication was that his contemporaries were challenging their elders. 'They're all doing what they want to do, not what's expected of them,' Lycett Green explained.

The company was set up on the princely sum of £6,000. Its name was chosen because it conjured up visions of dashing young men as well as being the cutting edge of a pair of tailor's scissors. It was also, coincidentally, the name of the gaming club pivotal to

Opposite For the original opening of Blades in Dover Street in 1962, Rupert Lycett Green wore a suit in Dormeuil fabric, made by tailor Eric Joy. Photograph: Fashion Museum, Bath.

Above Charles Hornby's suit for the Dover Street opening was also made by Eric Joy. Photograph: Fashion Museum, Bath.

the action in Ian Fleming's 1954 James Bond novel *Moonraker*, which would be filmed in 1964, so adding to its perceived pertinence. Foreseeing the shape of things to come, the logo selected for stationery and garment labels was a peacock.

The first item Blades sold was a chocolate-brown cashmere two-button jacket, but in spite of excellent social connections, business was slow. This may have been due to the fact that Blades was being run by untried young upstarts in a professional field as much as to the enterprise's intimidating, quasi-aristocratic image, or its dark-fronted premises that presented a daunting façade to the street. Even as it opened for business its reputation was grandiose: it was there to dress toffs. Rightly or wrongly, appearances seemed to imply that potential customers had to be wealthy and, in all probability, have a reference in *Burke's Peerage*.

The first year was not without unexpected adventures. All the clothes were stolen in a burglary and in a David and Goliath moment there was litigation with the formidable Sir Isaac Wolfson, whose powerful clothing empire encompassed Great Universal Stores.

Wolfson's GUS had launched an expensive television advertising campaign promoting a range of trousers called Blades and was committed contractually to running the campaign, only to be faced with Blades the tailors taking issue with the use of their registered name and threatening legal action. To Lycett Green's surprise and satisfaction, Wolfson eventually submitted to his challenge and although the television campaign continued, additional words were written into the text appearing on screen declaring that the trousers in the advertisement had no connection with Blades of Dover Street, the bespoke tailors. Good advertising at no cost to Blades, it would seem.

In 1964 Lycett Green married Candida Betjeman, daughter of writer and Poet Laureate John Betjeman, and on return from an extended motoring honeymoon in Europe decided, as he says, to take marital responsibilities seriously by working full-time in the business. The golden couple often featured jointly in the glossy magazines as glamorous young marrieds and rarely missed an opportunity to promote Blades and its forward-looking styling and tailoring. Naturally, most of Blades' wealthy customers were known socially to them both; they were friends, or men introduced by friends.

None the less the moment arrived when questions had to be asked about commercial viability. Hornby had already decided to depart to take up a richer life at Lloyds , and within two years Joy too had moved on, initially joining Mr Fish before setting up his own premises nearby. Joy's comment at this moment, recorded by Jonathan Aitken in *Young Meteors* (1967), makes

Above Duke of Windsor royal blue and white window-pane check suit, lemon cotton shirt, lemon and blue check Thai silk tie. Photograph: Bill King. Turnbull & Asser Archive.

waggish reading: 'I will make suits costing 50 guineas that will make their owners' marriages worth £50,000.'

Two solutions presented themselves. The first was to form a joint partnership with another company. The second was to move to a more suitable address, preferably with an imposing shop window; one that was a little closer to the hallowed ground of Savile Row, home to the world-famous bespoke tailors whom Lycett Green was challenging.

Discussions took place with the owners of a new shirt-making enterprise who were looking for premises in which to start up, but after extended meetings these plans came to naught. The enterprise was Mr Fish, headed by Michael Fish and Barry Sainsbury, which duly opened with a great flourish in Clifford Street, just off Savile Row.

Pursuing the second alternative, and with a new partner and a new team of tailors and cutters in harness, in March 1967 Lycett Green and Blades took up residence in a gracious Georgian building at 8 Burlington Gardens, elegantly and agreeably poised midway between Bond Street and Regent Street. The premises commanded a view of one end of Savile Row and looked disarmingly discreet, more like a town house or smart gentlemen's club.

Previously, as Mrs White's shop, the tall bay window had displayed hats, gloves, hunting stocks and handkerchiefs, but from now on, anyone passing would catch a glimpse of distinctive tailoring. Interior designer David Mlinaric was called in to create a sympathetic environment and stripped out every detail that was not original to the house, replacing it with very little, to create a light and airy space. There were open fires and leather armchairs. When Blades introduced its ready-to-wear collection, the clothes swung on clothes hangers from dress rails – an original idea when smart shops preferred to exhibit important items on display stands.

Under Lycett Green's direction the new cutters reflected the changing face of men's fashion. He wanted Blades' style to be unique, in his words to combine sharpness and elegance in exactly the right proportions. And soon Blades was challenging Savile Row's establishment at its own business, bringing in new design elements. With its impressive frontage, few men heading for their much-respected tailors in this tailoring heaven could miss the young upstart.

Blades' reputation grew on the provision of excellent, if expensive, bespoke tailoring. Lycett Green's regards his success as 'having helped bring young men back to Savile Row class bespoke tailoring'. Under his discerning eye, the clothes were custom-made to be comfortable while showing off a lean silhouette. A bespoke suit, which cost around £80, had a trim, slim jacket that

was free of the stiff, hand-stitched canvas linings and padding that made a traditional made-to-measure suit so distinctive. The jacket was cut with narrow sleeves and high armholes in order to emphasize the appearance of slimness and the trousers too were cut slimly to fit neatly. Soon the company was stealing some of the younger clientele that might once have gone to neighbouring tailors and its customer base grew steadily as class barriers faded and people became more socially mobile.

As competition from the new purveyors of Peacock finery increased in the neighbourhood, Lycett Green rose to the challenge. Even his friends at Mr Fish, now in business at the other end of the street, were majoring on tailoring – having taken on Eric Joy after his departure from Blades. Mr Fish's suits in soft colours and fabrics were in perfect harmony with the shop's extravagant shirts.

So with designs by Lycett Green, and to great peer group acclaim, Blades presented the first ever ready-to-wear men's fashion show in Savile Row. Ready-to-wear suits cost 50 guineas, sports jackets 28 guineas and trousers 10 guineas. Excellent press coverage followed and, as it happened, still more may well have been generated by an ensuing event. The show incurred the wrath of Edward Heath (who would become Prime Minister in 1970), who lived in a set of Albany chambers adjoining the shop. He demanded that 'the confounded row' be stopped as loud rock 'n'

roll music reverberated around Burlington Gardens while male models strutted the catwalk. It took skill to mollify the honourable Member of Parliament.

To be a Blades customer it was an advantage to be tall and slim like Lycett Green himself. Blades promoted the lean look, free of buttons, vents or crafty stitching that might add superfluous detailing. However, if you were not slim, Blades strived to make you appear so.

What made the clothes stand out were the choice of materials and the range of colours available. As well as classic tailoring in soft velvets there were clothes in wildly embroidered fabrics and vibrant tones. Lycett Green experimented with the unfamiliar, looking always for fabrics that were soft to the touch. If he heard that a French manufacturer was ending production of a particular velvet he liked, he would buy all the remaining lengths. Few of his fabric selections would fit the prescribed Savile Row image. Even the boots, made for Blades by Chelsea Cobbler, came in a variety of colours and Robert L. Green, fashion director of American *Esquire* and the first men's fashion editor to become internationally recognized, declared them to be Blades' signature item.

Looking back in 2009, Lycett Green, by then chairman of an oil exploration and production company, remained no less passionate about tailoring and the aims he and his partners had.

Opposite Kaffe Fassett, future tapestry designer, in luxurious, double-breasted, wolf coat, £393 15s, and lean suede trousers, £40 19s. *Men in Vogue*, Autumn/Winter 1969. Photograph: Peter Rand.

Above Jeremy Brett, actor, in white Indian silk dressing gown, silk lined and with exotic lapis lazuli and gold embroidery on cuffs and sides of hem, at Blades; 38gns. Fine hand-embroidered blue and green tapestry slippers, 30gns at Mr Fish. *Vogue*, November 1967. Photograph: Peter Rand.

He was particularly buoyed by an eminent Paris-based company asking, in 2008, for one of his early suit patterns to add to their menswear collection. Needless to say he had retained the patterns.

Everyone was complimentary about the first fashion show except for one journalist from Menswear trade magazine who was less than polite – and probably rightly so, I suppose. She thought I was young and arrogant. But once we had moved into ready-to-wear it really was a matter of trying to create what I thought people would want.

We wanted to make men's clothes sexy. We aimed to sell men clothes that women would like and find sexy. Men like clothes to attract women.

We used velvet, corduroy and flannel rather than worsted and mohair. The clothes felt good. Our strength was cut and finish. In fact our workmanship was excellent – maybe not as good as the great tailors like Huntsman or Anderson & Sheppard, but it was still good. Often we used same outworkers.

When Apple Corps, the Beatles' multimedia conglomerate, opened diagonally across the road at 3 Savile Row, pop groups and music industry luminaries became customers, all of them attracted by Blades' distinctive image. Script writers like Alan Simpson and Ray Galton became loyal customers.

Given Lycett Green's background, tailoring might have appeared to be an unusual business to enter. Especially without the requisite training at design school or art college and without an apprenticeship studying the cutting and sewing skills that mark a top tailor.

Maybe it is in the genes. My grandfather used to go to York races with three suits laid out in the back of the car for him to choose from, depending on the weather. And my great-uncle, Frank Green, used to take Lady Diana Cooper [the socialite and actress] to Paris – he would buy her anything she wanted as long as he approved. It wasn't a physical relationship – it was really a sartorial relationship.

I was always clothes-conscious. I liked clothes when I was a very small boy and used to go to parties in red silk shorts and a cream silk shirt thinking that all the girls would love me if I dressed nicely. Years later my stepmother used to dress me in my stepbrother's cast-off suits and although I liked him a lot, he was a year and a half older than me but shorter, so I was always wearing suits that were slightly too small. From that moment I understood that I could move around better if they were the right size and had changes made, like deeper armholes. I suppose I had discovered one of the mysteries of tailoring.

I had no previous connections with menswear before opening

Above Cream morning suit from Blades. The long jacket is double-breasted with covered buttons and wide lapels. Photograph: David Montgomery/Fashion Museum, Bath.

Blades. When I came back from Army service in 1956 I went to get a suit from Davies & Son and I bought a jacket in thick tweed. When I lifted my arms up the whole jacket rose to the top of my head because the armholes were in the wrong place and I thought, hang on, these boys don't really know what they are doing – although, to be honest, I think I was unlucky. They had an excellent older cutter I tried to tempt out of retirement for Blades. Was it Chanel who said the fit is all in the armholes?'

In the early 1950s, during Army service, Lycett Green cut quite a dash but remembers that if anyone wore anything unusual he was scowled at and the reaction seemed to be: what is that bounder wearing?

Two years later, however, if you looked smart they would probably have said: what a smart suit or shirt. If a remark of that sort had been made in the Army previously, it would have made one vaguely suspicious of odd tendencies in the person paying the compliment. It was the shortage of "birds" that made life competitive and made everyone think differently about dressing properly. It was just lucky we happened to start Blades at that time.

Of course, I didn't know then who the great Savile Row tailors were. It was only when providentially I met Eric Joy, who was thinking of setting up on his own, that Charles Hornby and I decided to open up our own business. What I wanted to do was produce slim-looking clothes; nothing startling in design but clothes that would be comfortable, like lightweight suits.

By 1969 Blades had established an outpost in New York. Like many successful London shops where visiting New Yorkers were popular customers, opening in America's capital city appeared to be natural progression. Nowhere, so it seemed then, would appreciate more London's skills and fashion strengths. The shop was perfectly positioned on Madison Avenue opposite another British outpost, the über-smart Annacat boutique owned by Lycett Green's London friends Janet Lyle and Maggie Keswick, whose richly romantic and glamorous clothes came from their Knightsbridge boutique. Annacat closed soon after Blades arrival. Blades lasted four years.

I've no excuses. I didn't know how to translate for America. I know now it was the wrong decision to do genuine bespoke tailoring in two cities, London and New York. If we had stuck to ready-to-wear it might have been different. Added to which New York was going through one of its major downturn periods with the stock market crash of 1973–4, the Vietnam War and Watergate.

In 1980, Lycett Green sold Blades as a going concern.

I sometimes think I was put out of business by people like Giorgio Armani. Not literally, of course. But while our clothes were well made and expensive, I just couldn't see how to diversify so as to compete effectively.

We were dressing men aged 30, but after the stock market crash the people who could afford our clothes were 40-plus. It was a small market and it had changed. When Armani styled Richard Gere for American Gigolo in 1980 in soft unstructured suits in muted colours, I was still working in bright colours. He made different, looser, lightweight suits and I was making fitted suits.

Many men who once came to Savile Row for craftsmanship were no longer interested in ordering a bespoke suit when they could buy an excellently made, beautiful one by Armani just by walking into a shop.

I thought, if Armani is going to be the man of the future, where am I? The writing was on the wall. I thought, this is the moment to get out. Otherwise I am going to have a bespoke, slim-suit, tailoring business and will be sitting here for 20 years waiting for the business to come back. I was 41 and still young enough to do something else.

But for Lycett Green the move to Savile Row from Dover Street had worked. At its peak Blades had a subtle influence on its neighbours and the way men dressed. Its quality, style and use of colour inspired other, younger tailors and spawned a number of boutiques, which attempted with varying degrees of success to go upmarket in search of the man who might have shopped at Blades. When men admit to the places where they buy their clothes it is a sure sign of success, and men wearing clothes from Blades were quick to do so. Blades' clothes were worn with pride, not simply because of their social pedigree or the implication that to own them you must be wealthy, but because they were underscored with good taste. This was particularly true of Blades' velvet suits – instantly and distinctively noticeable, and for anyone without one, covetable.

Opposite Both formal and casual velvet suits formed a major part of Blades' annual collections. Trousers were flared; shirts and ties were often in Liberty prints. 1969. Photograph: *Evening Standard*/Getty Images.

MICHAEL FISH AND BARRY SAINSBURY

Mr Fish

CLIFFORD STREET

Situated in Clifford Street, midway between Savile Row and Bond Street, Mr Fish was an expensive, richly vibrant emporium, one eminently suited to Peacocks. Perfectly in tune with its clientele, a heady mixture of aristocrats and show biz luminaries in pursuit of sartorial emancipation, it was possibly the most internationally famous, upmarket designer-boutique of its day.

Headed by Michael Fish, the shop's clothes were colourful, luxurious and well-made, driven by Fish's own low-key consuming passion for good-looking clothes. He was welcoming, gregarious and star-struck, with a natural charm that came with a sense of self-deprecating humour; he turned customers into friends and friends into customers. He was also, as it happened, adept at greeting, then amiably manipulating, journalists from press and television, promoting himself as well as the shop. It was a fortuitous combination.

The shop opened to considerable anticipation in December 1967, just in time to reap the benefits of the Christmas spending spree – which it did handsomely. And it was not long before Fish, as well as his clothes, were being seen at many of London's smart events. Soon his clientele would include Noel Coward (who adored a lavish pink silk dressing-gown shot with gold, a gift from Vivien Leigh), Sammy Davis Jnr, James Fox, Duke Ellington, Lord Montagu of Beaulieu, Lord Snowdon, Rock Hudson and innumerable actors from the London stage. Among the women were Princess Margaret, Lady Harlech, Evangeline Bruce and Vanessa Redgrave, who were buying gifts for others or ordering shirts for themselves. Mama Cass ordered kaftans. For Muhammad Ali's 'Rumble in the Jungle' fight against George Foreman in Zaire in 1974 he designed the dressing-gown Ali wore to enter the ring. And for Picasso, he made special shirts for which the artist rewarded him with drawings to decorate the shop and a dedicated, then ornamented, copy of a slim book entitled *Picasso Designs 1966–1967*. As Fish would often say: 'Not bad for a boy from Wood Green'.

Born in Essex in 1940, Michael Fish had no formal education. He started work earning £3 10s a week aged 15, as the boy who cleaned the glass counter-tops with methylated spirits at Colletts in Shaftsbury Avenue, on the corner of Wardour Street. The shop was owned by Sir Henry Collett, whose brother was Mayor of the City of London. Colletts had a particular appeal for Fish because among its selections of imported American clothes were button-down shirts, the like of which he had never seen before. To the young Fish these were the pinnacle of style.

As he became familiar with London's clothes shops, so Fish gravitated upmarket. He next worked at the Jermyn Street Shirtmaker; then, progressing to greater heights, he moved to New & Lingwood before arriving at Turnbull & Asser, where he would help turn the company into the most adventurous shirt-maker in Jermyn Street and an integral part of the Peacock shopping

Opposite Michael Fish, man in a white suit, double-breasted and with wide lapels, with brightly coloured and patterned cotton shirt and silk Kipper tie. Photograph: Roy Jones. Private collection.

circuit. It was here he rejoined Kenneth Williams who, in earlier years at Colletts, had been delegated the task of training him. It was an auspicious reunion that would lead to Turnbull's launching of the first-ever ready-made shirts in a street that was, until then, known only for making shirts to measure. It led to the rise of Turnbull's fortunes. With Fish's youthful precocity in full drive, the company became both famous and flamboyant, with new young customers drawn in by colourful displays never before seen in the windows of Jermyn Street's bespoke shirt shops.

Looking back, as chairman of Turnbull & Asser, Williams says now: 'Michael was full of ideas and key to taking Turnbull ahead of the competition while maintaining Turnbull's values'. Shirts and ties began to explode with colour. There were more fabrics to choose from, silks and satins, even frills if you wanted them. As for ties, each time a new batch was ordered Fish increased the width and the Kipper tie, the symbol of the 1960s, was born.

Fish spent nine years at Turnbull & Asser, during which time he polished his skills – and it was while he was there that his future business partner, Barry Sainsbury, suggested that the time was ripe to launch a new shop selling expensive, high quality men's clothes. It was to be at the top end of the social scale, well away from the middle-class niche carved out by Carnaby Street where, coincidentally, in his self-imposed apprenticeship, Fish had worked briefly as an assistant to John Stephen (see p.40–5).

With Sainsbury's smart family and social connections, and with the customers who followed Fish into his new emporium, the shop was an immediate social success. An upmarket haberdashers, it was often called, but what an enjoyable place to be and to look at clothes. The shelves were generously packed with brightly coloured silk and cotton shirts that billowed rather than clung to the body like most shirts in the mid-1960s; exuberantly wide ties; cashmere sweaters; and dandified velvet jackets that were often elegantly draped, double-breasted with one-button and long-roll lapels. Winged back seaming ensured that the jackets fitted the back sleekly. There were also luxurious dressing-gowns in hand-printed, extravagantly heavy silks that cost eye-watering amounts of money.

For anyone aspiring to be a Peacock or wealthy enough not to consider the prices, Mr Fish was perfect. The shop broke new ground. The prices may have been high – a white brocade jacket was £35, for example, and a black voile roll-neck shirt £8 – but so was the quality and, due to the shop's social cachet the clothes were non-judgementally considered to be in adventurous good taste. Mr Fish had created an instantly recognizable pedigree that fitted in with the shop's slogan, to be found on their handkerchiefs and carrier bags: 'Peculiar to Mr Fish'.

If some men were initially slow to shop there, women were not, often rushing in determined to buy husbands or lovers something

Opposite Peter Menegas, writer, in Mr Fish's definitive chocolate brown velvet dungarees with lacings at the chest. Photograph: Peter Rand, 1970.

Above In the beginning: Sean Connery in a fitting with Michael Fish at Turnbull & Asser. Turnbull & Asser Archive.

bright and fashionable to match the mood of the clothes they were buying for themselves. To them a distinctive Mr Fish shirt and tie was all it took to make a man look right and, within months, men who had never considered fashion a part of their lives were shopping there. British designers like Ossie Clark wore Mr Fish; so did leading foreign designers like Rome's Valentino and New York's Geoffrey Beene.

The shop quickly developed a wealthy gay following, too, for whom Michael Fish, his staff and the boutique's trend-setting image was liberating. Fish targeted London's smartest set – especially anyone newly successful in the arts, theatre or cinema with a taste for dressing-up – and his clothes were photographed constantly for the fashion pages of *Vogue* and *Harpers & Queen*.

By November 1969 Anthony King-Deacon was able to report in *The Times*: 'Mr Fish is a phenomenon of our age. He is a product of the 1960s sartorial revolution. His shop is probably the axle around which spins that particular, exclusive type of fashion associated with the swinging aristocracy – the suave velvet suits and incredible lace shirts. The rich, the famous and the anonymously important people who shop there do so at the risk of rubbing shoulders with those hangers on who think they are rich, famous and important. The shop is, in fact, a way of life, an equivalent to a Pall Mall Club where the assistants have names and the clients sign bills.'

The key to Fish's success was an appreciation of luxury fabrics and an innate understanding of what each might or might not do if turned into men's clothing. He was ready to take risks when looking for new ideas with potential. Not all of them worked, of course. But he did take Jermyn Street's standard high collared shirt and, by making the points slightly longer and more widely spread, and then teaming the shirt with a large-knot tie, gave it a fresher, peculiarly Mr Fish, appearance. Ties and shirts, it seemed, had never looked so good. As for scarves and pocket handkerchiefs, he had thick silks specially hand-blocked and printed. Fabrics had become a passion.

Mr Fish outfits captured the Peacock need to be different. Well documented moments, such as the time Mick Jagger was clothed in a white moiré frilly dress, inspired by the ceremonial military uniform of the Evzones (or light infantry) in Athens, for a free Rolling Stones concert in Hyde Park in 1969, and David Bowie was dressed in a long blue printed silk dress for the original cover of *The Man Who Sold the World* (1970), only served to cement his reputation. Both outfits touched on Peacock notions of vanity – 'look at me' – and brought massive press coverage to the blossoming rock stars as well as Fish himself.

There were also joint shows with Mary Quant, Valentino and many others. With so much going right, it seemed the shop could not fail. But fail it did.

Opposite Muhammad Ali in dressing-gown designed by Michael Fish for Ali's entry into the ring in 'the Rumble in the Jungle' challenge against George Foreman in Zaire, October 1974. Private collection.

The key to Michael Fish's success was also the key to Mr Fish's demise: extravagance. It was simple; the company over-reached itself. While it was a great success publicly, it was not making the money it should have been. As Rudi Patterson, who worked for Fish, remarked to me in June 2009, 'Fabrics were too expensive, even in those days. He spent too much. Everything was extravagant, even his shows were extravagances.'

There was a moment of reprieve, however. Sainsbury withdrew from the company in 1969 and in stepped Captain Fred Barker, landowner and heir to the Singer Sewing Machine fortune, who was married to Venetia Quarry, stepdaughter of Lord Mancroft.

Angus McGill recorded Captain Barker's entrance into the fashion arena in the *Evening Standard*: 'He brought much needed new capital to the aid of Mr Fish, the most celebrated of all the fashion houses, a highly successful business which, in spite of a turnover of more than a quarter of a million pounds a year, was actually losing money.

Now he is Michael Fish's full partner and to the surprise of some customers has imposed more positive financial controls on such mundane matters as sending out bills.

Michael Fish is planning even more extravagant fashions as a result. Captain Barker is pleased.

But the Captain cannot have been pleased for long as soon he, too, would bale out having called a halt to the need for further injections of money into the shop.

The trade magazine *Menswear* gushed that Mr Fish 'has probably had more famous names through its doors than the Savoy has served smoked salmon'. But then it asked the question, 'What went wrong? If you count not making a profit going wrong – and most would – then something certainly did go wrong. In its five years the shop never made a profit'.

The answer lay in the fact that the often sumptuous fabrics used, which were exclusive to Mr Fish, cost so much to produce in small quantities that they could not be rationally priced, even in this expensive haven. Without sufficient turnover to cover the value of stock held in the shop's basement, the revenue never matched expectations and the business ceased to be viable. None of this was helped by the considerable number of customers who had taken advantage of the bonhomie and personal service provided by Fish. Long-term credit and bad debts – often as customers traded on their friendship with Fish – had also got out of hand.

Fierce parallel competition was now being driven by an expanding fashion industry, professionally run by people with commercial experience. Allied to these factors was the imminent

Opposite Mr Fish evening shirts came in all manner of colours and shapes. Two examples worn by Michael Fish (left) and Barry Sainsbury (right). *Sunday Times*, 15 September 1968. Photograph: Clive Arrowsmith / Fashion Museum, Bath.

Opposite One of Michael Fish's rollneck shirts that would redefine the boudaries of formal dress for men. 1969. Private collection.

Above A white kaftan for a man to wear about the house, credited in a Mr Fish fashion show as a 'smoking dress'. 1969. Private collection.

Above Barry Sainsbury with son Sebastian in dashing wool gabardine roan pink suit, 38gns to measure. Silk crepon shirt with deep collar, 9gns. Kipper tie 3gns. All at Mr Fish. *Vogue*, June 1967. Photograph: Patrick Lichfield.

Opposite Michael Fish, on the steps of Mr Fish in Clifford Street in long leather coachman's coat and leather bush hat. 1970. Photograph: Jon Lyons/Rex Features.

expiry of the shop's lease and an anticipated leap in rent. Captain Barker decided Mr Fish would cease trading; the shop would close. The days when an easy-going, socially active enthusiast could hope to sustain teams of tailors and seamstresses making remarkable clothes on the basis of erratic shop-keeping was over. A 'Drastic Sale' took place. With prices never before so low, everything sold.

In public Michael Fish remained optimistically buoyant and there was a brief resurrection of the business in Mount Street, with new partners that included impresarios Robert Stigwood and David Shaw. Fish was quoted in an interview in the 'Money News' column of the *Evening News* as saying: 'This time there will be no credit. Obviously you can't say to someone like the Marquis of Dufferin and Ava – sorry old chap, no goodies without the cash – so we'll have to have accounts. The accountant will take my mind off money worries and the staff will be as honest as the Festival of Light'.

But for all the good intentions, Mr Fish was never resuscitated. A fire consumed the new premises in 1974 as Britain battled with recession. The new backers could see little future in retailing expensive clothes during an economic downturn. Fish then lent his presence and address book to the short-lived Embassy nightclub in Old Bond Street, opened by Jeremy Norman as London's equivalent of New York's Studio 54.

In the pantheon of the fashion gods of London's Swinging Sixties, Michael Fish's name fits comfortably alongside those of Mary Quant, Jean Muir, Zandra Rhodes, Bill Gibb and Ossie Clark. His off-Savile Row emporium, with its highly prized clothes, helped make upmarket men's fashion what it was at its defining moment: world renowned.

Opposite A fashionable pair in evening wear: Janet Lyle of Annacat and Michael Fish of Mr Fish. *The Sunday Times*, 11 February 1968. Photograph: David Montgomery/Fashion Museum, Bath.

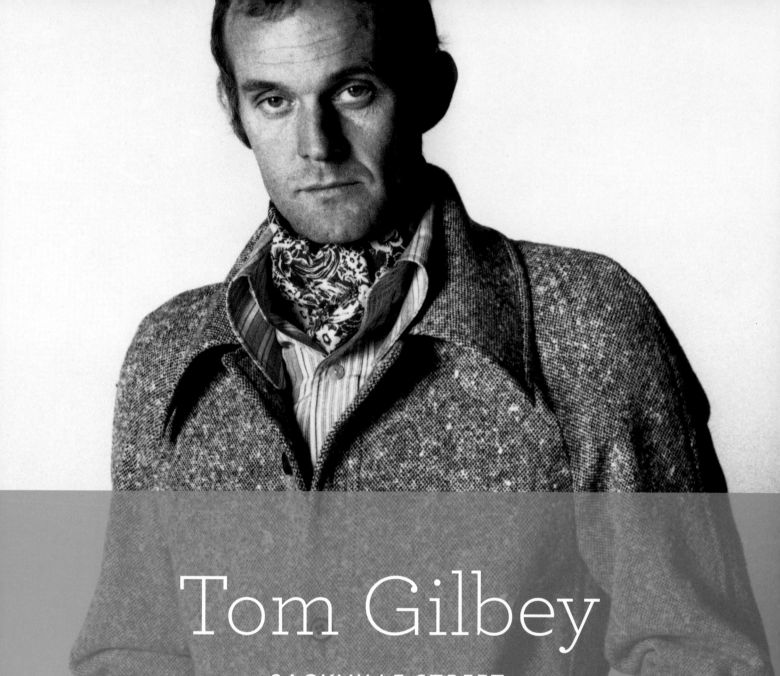

Tom Gilbey

SACKVILLE STREET

With supreme confidence, Tom Gilbey formally opened his studio at 36 Sackville Street in 1967 with the presentation of his first couture collection. It was, he announced, based on 'pace age' (note, not 'space age', which was Pierre Cardin's promotional angle), which meant that all the clothes were lightweight and interchangeable in order to have a multi-purpose life. There were safari suits, jump suits, blouson jackets and shorts.

At 29, he was one of the first of a new generation of designers with experience in both design and tailoring attempting to make his mark.

Building up to this momentous event Gilbey had done his own form of apprenticeship and understood the clothing business in fine detail, from fabric design to sales at the shop counter. Hence his confidence. As he said in 1967 in an interview with me: 'If you want to be a successful designer you must know the business thoroughly.' And from his studio he planned to run a design consultancy in addition to his couture work. Within four years of the opening, *Men in Vogue* declared he was 'Britain's one and only home grown couturier for men.'

Looking at Gilbey's curriculum vitae, every move appears part of a natural but determined progression leading to the couture business and design consultancy; the result a foregone conclusion. First he studied art and design at Sir John Cass College (1961–2)

in Commercial Road, east London, and then polished his craft by working on the bench with tailors in the East End, before heading for Wuppertal in Germany, to work with textile manufacturers and learn about fabrics (1963). From there it was back to England for a period working for the multiple tailors John Temple and Neville Reed, acting as their liaison with Pierre Cardin in Paris. Cardin, having assumed the mantle of the world's first major designer of men's clothes, had just signed an agreement to create a small collection for the Neville Reed shops. Gilbey went to the factories Cardin used in order to study the Frenchman's designs and to introduce Cardin's cutting style to England.

From Neville Reed Gilbey went to work with Dougie Millings in 1965 (see p.46–7), famed for being 'the tailor to the stars', whose roster of clients was almost entirely from the show biz world. Millings' own defining moment had come earlier when he created the Beatles' Cardin-like suits with collarless jackets, the outfits that gave them the boyish image that rocketed them to international fame. With this step in his apprenticeship achieved and his career trajectory firmly fixed, he then approached John Michael Ingram, already a driving force in men's fashion with his John Michael shops, proposing to help set up a fashion design consultancy for Ingram in 1966.

With his abundant energy and drive, Gilbey soon wanted more. 'Even at school I was interested in clothes. I liked to stand out. I

Opposite Tom Gilbey in his favourite raglan-sleeved, belted Donegal tweed jacket, £135. *Evening Standard*, 28 February 1972. Photograph: Roy Jones.
Overleaf, page 120 For Gilbey's 1971 collection, slim suits were teamed with hand-knit Op Art wool sweaters in monochromatic geometric patterns. Private collection.

Overleaf, page 121 In the 1971 collection, melton donkey jackets and blousons were either trimmed with black or had brightly coloured overlocked edges. Stud fastenings and bellows patch pockets provided additional detail. Private collection.

always did something different. I was never embarrassed. I never blushed. I wanted to see my name on labels. As I was already picking up my own consultancy contracts, which gave me an income, it was time to set up on my own.'

So in 1967, with an overflowing belief in his own abilities, Gilbey moved into premises in Sackville Street, midway between Savile Row and Piccadilly, as if challenging the grandees of tailoring. 'Savile Row can't design,' he is quoted as saying to Rodney Bennett-England, in his 1967 book *Dress Optional*. 'They can make superb clothes [but] what they need more than anything else now are designers. The basic suit has lasted fifty years. It has reached its ultimate in design.' And although he may not have had the social connections that sped his equally upstart competitors like Blades and Mr Fish forward, in no time his clients were as varied as theirs and included the fashion-minded Duke of Bedford and pop groups like the Kinks and the Animals. His skill was now being recognized. And his name was indeed on the labels: Tom Gilbey Couturier / Design London / W1.

'I opened what I believe was the first men's couture house in the world, dealing with the avant-garde rather than the traditional Savile Row suit,' he recalls. 'If any of my clients wanted such a suit, I would have sent them to Huntsman or Anderson & Sheppard.' As he fought against the stiff formality and the conservatism of the day, claiming as often as he could that you could still be

well-dressed and not wear a tie when going into a restaurant, hotel or Pall Mall club, and that an aristocrat in jeans was still an aristocrat, he never lost sight of his aims or altered his convictions. He was committed to the cause of subtle design changing the way men dressed and worked hard to introduce fresh ideas to his customers and to the companies where he was a design consultant, always attempting to challenge preconceived conceptions about the function of men's clothes. Alongside Pierre Cardin and Britain's Hardy Amies he was among the first to licence his name with leading manufacturers (and the first to do so in Germany).

Gilbey's skill lay in his ability to take an idea and develop it using strong, clean lines, following his own tenets of function and creativity. He put zips on sports jackets and pockets, recreated the wrap-and-tie coat and introduced soft pleated trousers that measured 22 inches (56cm) at the turn-ups. His knitwear patterns were inspired by Gustav Klimt. He turned anoraks and windcheaters into sophisticated blousons. All his clothes seemed to reflect his own interest in sport, allowing for physical mobility.

For all Gilbey's dedication and success, and the possibility that he really was the world's first couturier for men, his was possibly the least known designer name in Britain during the Peacock days. Yet he had an important presence in both Europe and America, where his design skills and talent for self-promotion within the menswear industry helped him play an important

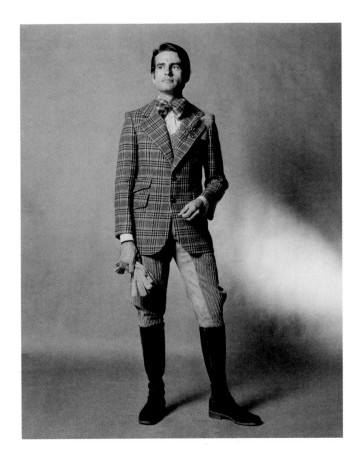

consultancy role with leading manufacturers, into whose ranges he injected what was perceived as London fashion expertise. He had contracts with major producers such as Ahlers and Bäumler in Germany and Littlewoods in England. He created outfits for Elton John in 1973, designed uniforms for hotels and smart restaurants, and worked with giant corporations on a number of commercial projects. As Richard Compton Miller wrote a decade later in the first edition of *Who's Really Who* (1983), Gilbey was 'Britain's answer to Pierre Cardin, Ralph Lauren and Calvin Klein. His is perfectionist work'.

Gilbey's personal dress sense was an indication of the way he wanted men's clothes to go. He said, 'I'm slightly balding and athletic. Most people think I'm a dancer or choreographer or an actor rather than a designer, which influences the way I dress. I try for clean sporty looks or hard dramatic ones.' Gilbey reached his fashion nirvana by wearing only four basic colours: blue, cream, black and grey.

In 1974 Gilbey was quoted by Lendal Scott Ellis in *Harpers & Queen* as saying: 'Every man should have the equivalent of a little black dress so he can change the look of it.' He then expanded this Peacock moment by explaining that it was important for a man to add touches of the dandy with coloured belts and scarves. He also suggested lapel pins – something ornamental, but not a brooch.

After 20 years in Sackville Street Gilbey moved his business to New Burlington Street, where he found additional activity creating exclusive waistcoats that were worn by Prince William, amongst others, hence his soubriquet – the Waistcoat King. Then, as repairing clauses made a Mayfair base prohibitively expensive, he quietly bowed out.

'I felt that after many years of a hugely varied career with clients ranging from royalty, aristocracy, pop stars and footballers to corporate companies like ICI and Dupont, as well as being involved with film and theatre – and also having been a true innovator of fashion – I was no longer enjoying it.' Golf and tennis, however, he does.

Above Traditional hacking jacket trimmed with suede, £94, teamed with corduroy and suede patched jodhpurs, £35. Both to order at Tom Gilbey. Rust suede boots, £32 to measure at Chelsea Cobbler, Sackville Street. *Evening Standard*, 28 February 1972. Photograph: Roy Jones/*Evening Standard*/ Hulton Archive/Getty Images.

Above Jay Johnson, one of Andy Warhol's superstars, in zip-up battle-dress and baggies in multi-check cotton from Gilbey's mid-season collection. £87 to order. *Evening Standard*, 22 March 1972. Photograph: Roy Jones/*Evening Standard*/Hulton Archive/Getty Images.

Doug Hayward

MOUNT STREET

Never a part of Savile Row's select brotherhood, Doug Hayward was none the less a friend of the hallowed square mile of tailoring establishments because he was never viewed as its direct competition. His clientele was made up of the newly successful 1960s fashion-minded elite, Peacocks in the making, all drawn from the worlds of the arts, media, cinema and theatre. These were men who by the nature of their professions were disinterested in the fusty ways of Savile Row, preferring instead to seek a tailor living their kind of lifestyle. Hayward was such a man.

Television chat show host Michael Parkinson summed up his amiability and skills succinctly in his autobiography *Parky* (2008): 'Hayward's shop in Mount Street was a salon for actors, photographers, landed gentry, soccer players, racing drivers, models, royalty and associated layabouts, all of them chosen and approved by a remarkable lad who left school at 15 and became one of the great stylists of the Sixties and onwards.' Naturally all these men would wear their Hayward suits when interviewed on his television programme and Parkinson himself, a lifelong friend and customer, would wear one too.

Hayward was a man of infinite charm and a tailor of distinction. Until he set up on his own, he was in partnership with tailor Dimi Major in Fulham, south-west London. As Major Hayward, the duo were much respected as tailors and renowned for the excellence of their craft as well as the new-style cut of their suits. They had a broad club-like spectrum of young customers, many of them fledgling actors like Terence Stamp, who wanted custom-made suits but considered a visit to a Savile Row tailor an anathema, both socially and financially.

Like many others setting up in business in London in the early 1960s, Hayward was fired with ambition. He needed success. Coming from Hounslow he wanted to be a first-class Mayfair tailor, making, as he often said, 'suits that fit', in direct competition to Savile Row where suits, he believed, were 'shapes disguising the body beneath, not shapes cut to enhance the man by making him look slim, relaxed and comfortable.'

Hayward's talent lay in having clear ideas as to how each individual should dress, but he was a tailor by trade and inclination, not a fashion designer. So his suits had a fluid signature shape, neither tight nor loose, with minimal lining in the jackets. There were no extraneous details, no eccentric or fancy embellishments. As he said memorably of his own customers, almost every one of them famous: 'They all look a mixture of smart but scruffy in suits that are beautifully made.'

Hayward's suits had a distinctive pedigree that was evident in the high quality cloths used and the ease with which a man wore them. In his suits men did indeed look slim, or at least comfortable with their size – a fact that appealed particularly to

Opposite Doug Hayward, celebrity tailor, in comfortable beige Moygashel linen suit, £60. 'I like to see suits with individual looks so that if ten men wearing my suits were lined up along a wall you couldn't tell I had dressed them. I often talk someone out of having a suit rather than make one that will turn out looking rotten.' *Town*, August 1967. Photograph: Peter Rand.

actors. Many clients claimed that a Hayward jacket would make you look as if you had lost pounds. Hayward himself was tall and well built, a big man who never looked it.

Leaving school at 15, Hayward was encouraged to learn a trade, preferably one where you kept your hands clean. So he began his career as a trainee tailor, learning to cut and sew men's suiting fabrics in Shepherd's Bush. He might then have applied to join a Savile Row company but was warned that with his accent he would never be front of house and would always be in the cutting rooms at the back. Undeterred, he knew his time would come.

While working in partnership with Dimi Major he built up an impressive client base but, in 1963, at the venerable age of 28, Major and Hayward came to an amicable separation. While Major preferred to remain in Fulham's unharried pastures, Hayward wanted the challenge of competing with the deity in Savile Row. He struck out on his own (saying in later years that he looked back on his partnership with Major as the happiest years of his life).

His first move was to take a small room in Pall Mall (a cubby hole, is how he described it), where he sat for weeks with a pile of fabric swatches and a telephone, wondering if he had made a grievous mistake. Nothing happened. Then one day the telephone rang; it was Terence Stamp, his Fulham client, looking for him. Word spread that Hayward was still in business and soon he was doing

his tailor's rounds with his swatches, in a secondhand Mini, calling at homes or at hotels like The Dorchester in Park Lane, a favourite of Hollywood actors. One client placed an order for ten suits.

His moment had come, and when in 1967 he opened his premises in Mayfair in 1967, at 89 Mount Street, just paces from the grand Connaught Hotel, it seemed as if overnight he had created a meeting place, a club-like retreat, where he could discreetly suit actors like John Mills, Michael Caine (whom he would dress for his 1969 film *The Italian Job*) and Roger Moore (who would wear Hayward's dark suits as James Bond), actors for whom a Savile Row showroom would be no fun at all. In no time, with friends like Patrick Lichfield, he was involved in a real club when, together, they opened Burke's in Clifford Street in December 1969, a restaurant club that became instantly – and fashionably – crowded.

'Doug had friends who became customers and customers who became friends,' says Audie Charles, who initially joined Hayward to help run the small tailoring business in May 1967. Having taken time off for her family, she returned to work alongside Hayward, with charm and efficiency, for a further 25 years until Hayward's death in 2008, and continues to keep the business operational. In conversation, she recalls:

Doug chose not to be on Savile Row because he wanted to do it his way. He had a different attitude. He was born humble and had

Above In the shop: Tommy Steele with Doug Hayward. Steele wears a casual single-breasted corduroy suit, 60 gns, teamed with 1960s fashionable rollneck sweater. *Daily Telegraph Magazine*, 5 April 1968. Photograph: Hans Feurer.

worked very happily in Fulham, but when he moved into town it had to be on his terms, not on the Row's. Their way was not his way.

In Savile Row someone will sell you a suit and help select a fabric; then you see a fitter. At Hayward's the atmosphere was intimate, with Doug and the fitter always present. His service was incredibly personal – you got to know Doug, he got to know you ... Of course, those were the days when actors and directors and photographers seemed to care about clothes and have money; Peacocks in their own way. Now it is a business crowd, investment bankers, people in finance. Only the occasional actor. The business crowd need things custom-made. Everywhere you go in the world there are the same shops, the same labels, the same brands; the one original thing you can have when you have money is a bespoke suit. You can have it as you wish.

In a sense Hayward tailoring was safe, not adventurous. His [Doug's] knack was to give a man a suit that he could put on and forget about, knowing that he looked good. He didn't want anyone to say, there goes a Hayward suit; he wanted you to know the man looked good but you weren't quite sure why.

When the shop opened it was sparsely furnished but smart. It was designed by Ciancimino to look starkly simple. Only a suede coat thrown over a sofa injected informality. A few ties were on view, and some pieces of luggage; the tailoring was at the back.

We started doing Hayward Classics in the front of the shop, thinking everyone needs a blue cashmere sweater, a striped shirt and things like that. So we used the window to draw people in and introduced ranges of sweaters, shirts, dressing-gowns and umbrellas. Everything, in fact, that Doug and his friends would like to own. He had an eye for line and colour that was distinctive and this worked as well for a shirt, a suit or an armchair. Somehow you knew it was right. It brought in new customers.

There was talk of expanding the business, perhaps another tailoring shop. But Doug said he could not be in two businesses at once. There were offers from a New York store, asking him to create a special venture with them, but he turned down this opportunity, too, believing he would have little control over what was happening while he was based in London.

Tailoring was what he understood and enjoyed. His was not the formality of Savile Row, though he knew the people in the tailoring world of Savile Row, of course, and the other people dressing the London Peacocks like Mr Fish, Tommy Nutter, Blades and Turnbull & Asser. But he was not concerned with fashion's daily workings.

It was said he was fortunate that as well as being charming, a good raconteur and amusing, he could make a good suit. His business in Mount Street is the proof of that.

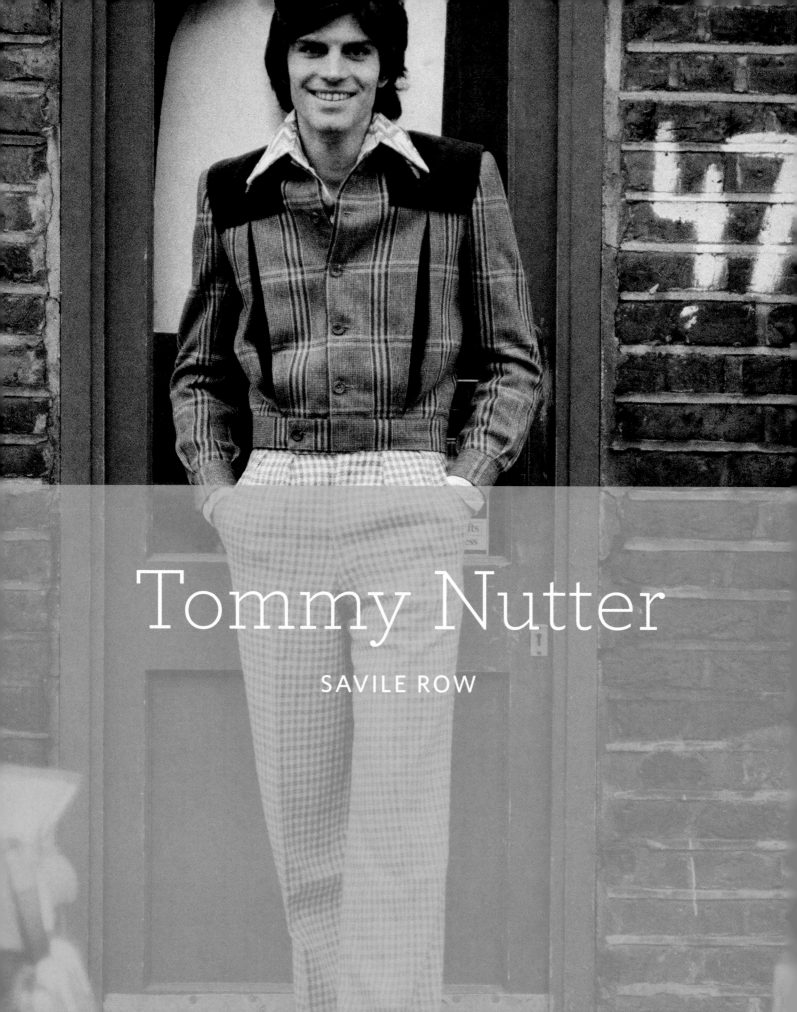

Tommy Nutter

SAVILE ROW

By the time Nutters of Savile Row opened on Valentine's Day 1969, its success was all but guaranteed; London's world of entertainment had been alerted. Cilla Black, at that time known as the Beatles' best friend and the songbird from Liverpool rather than the adored television personality she would become, had already announced to the *Sunday Express* that she was backing a tailor who was setting-up in Savile Row. 'It is going to be terribly posh,' she trilled. 'There will be none of the common gimmicks of Carnaby Street, and no gaudy décor. All the suits will be made on straightforward, classical lines. We hope to cater for lords, ambassadors and royalty. I particularly want to have something made for Lord Snowdon. This is my first venture into the rag trade. In the past I have been advised against it ... I am putting a large amount of money into this – but I do not want to say how much. I think Tommy Nutter is the best tailor in London.'

Joining her in this sartorial debut with his own financial investment was Peter Brown, friend and personal assistant of Brian Epstein and the Beatles. As he was on the board of Apple Corps, the Beatles' company he had helped establish, his additional responsibility would be drawing celebrities into the establishment.

Nutter, then 26, was not a tailor by profession, but in a seven-year apprenticeship with a Savile Row tailor prior to this momentous day, he had absorbed the essential lore and rules of the traditional British gentleman's classic wardrobe. In his new role, heading a

tailoring establishment, he would prove that he had also developed a clear vision for identifying those subtle changes to traditional style, which, however simple, had the impact of a fashion statement. Nutters of Savile Row's tailoring would soon stand out.

After leaving Willesden Technical College aged 16 in 1959, Nutter started work as a trainee draughtsman, but hated it. So his parents suggested that he enter the Civil Service and, on passing the entrance exams, he found himself appointed as a Clerical Officer at the Ministry of Works. His duties, he discovered, were centred on making the office tea. He hated that, too.

'I kept thinking I had an aptitude for clothes,' he said in an interview with me (*Evening Standard*, 14 March 1973), 'and then I saw an advertisement in the *Evening Standard* for a tailor's assistant at Donaldson, Williams & Ward in the Burlington Arcade. I rushed to get it.' It was a life-changing moment and would instill in him a respectful knowledge of the tailor's craft and skills. It was while here that he met cutter Edward Sexton, who would join him to become a fellow director when Nutters was established.

In fact it was Michael Fish who played an instrumental part in his ascendancy. Nutter had earlier approached him for a job. The shop had the kind of glamorous clientele and fashion direction he aspired to. But instead of employing him, Fish encouraged him

Opposite Tweed mix: jacket with toning cord shoulder patches and insets, £75, and co-ordinating check trousers, £35 at Nutters. *Evening Standard*, 15 March 1972. Photograph: Roy Jones/*Evening Standard*/ Hulton Archive/Getty Images

to find the requisite backing and open his own workrooms – echoing the route he himself had taken in order to establish Mr Fish. The wheels were set in motion.

With backers finally in place, and with Edward Sexton participating in the venture, the newly fledged company took premises in Savile Row. The small shop was on the wrong side of the street, Nutter was told, but it had a window facing London's pre-eminent tailors so, to the partners, this seemed an eminently acceptable proposition. Their presence, they confidently believed, would make their side of the road as important as the other. Joining them to add their craftsmen's skills to the enterprise were Roy Chittleborough and Joseph Morgan, tailors who had trained with two of Savile Row's finest houses: Kilgour, French & Stanbury and Davies & Son. The shyly charming, ever-smiling, ever-boyish Nutter was the photogenic face of the upstart enterprise.

It was a bold venture, with the grandees on the Row watching every move. While a number of traditionalists said privately they believed the business would flounder within a year, younger tailors working there wished him luck, hoping he would enliven the bespoke suit trade and introduce a different type of customer to the street.

In no time the newcomers had assembled all the outward trappings required by young pretenders. Their premises were

small but discreet, their service unctuous enough to pass for Establishment regulation behaviour and the tailoring itself, as it was to prove, was unmistakably excellent. Better still, the designs were noticeably more fashionable and daring than they were traditional – traditional was not what Tommy Nutter's clients wanted or expected of him. Within four years he would be considered as important as any British tailor or designer. A lone voice in this Establishment world, he would reconcile the traditions of Savile Row with Peacock flair.

With their youthful confidence, Nutter and Sexton aimed to create impeccable tailoring but, driven by ambition, they wanted to extend their impact by adding a recognizable visual dash that would separate them from their neighbouring competitors. Nutter's idea was to rework conservative classic styles in 'younger' fabrics and shapes and, occasionally, mix complementary fabric patterns in one garment. A jacket therefore might have an insert of a different pattern on its front but the effect was sympathetic because the two fabrics used were in identical colour tones. The effect was distinctively Nutters. To emphasize a jacket's impact, often its edges were subtly braided – even when it was in tweed. Jackets, generally, were slightly shorter in length with square shoulders and narrow sleeves but no vent.

Tall, slender Nutter was himself perfect for projecting the Nutters image. 'Someone once told me I was the best model I could have.

Above Hardy Amies, couturier, in grey flannel suit, made to his design at Nutters. *Evening Standard*, 31 January 1973. Photograph: Roy Jones/*Evening Standard*/Getty Images.

Opposite Tim Rice with Andrew Lloyd Webber. Rice in gaberdine dinner suit, £180, Lloyd Webber in plum coloured frock coat, £240, both to measure at Nutters. *Evening Standard*, 8 August 1973. Photograph: Roy Jones/*Evening Standard*/Getty Images.

It sounds bigheaded, but it works,' the shy Nutter admitted. 'The best way for people to see the clothes is being worn, in close-up.' So everywhere he went he was dressed impeccably in Nutters' finery. In 1971, years before he ever set foot there, he was regarded as a fashion force in New York and featured on Best Dressed lists alongside a number of his clients. The *New York Times* claimed he was the original architect of the new bespoke movement while *American Menswear* magazine reported that his image was tradition spiced with daring.

Nutter was discreet about naming clients but the PR machinery that came with his backers ensured that his national and international clients were soon acknowledged as such in the press, wearing his clothes. There was Bianca Jagger's wedding suit, which was made for her marriage to Mick; a man's tweed suit, made specially for Twiggy, in which she looked stunning; and, of course, suits made for the Beatles, three of which were worn for the cover of the 1969 album *Abbey Road* (George Harrison elected to wear denims). Andrew Lloyd Webber and Tim Rice had evening clothes made, inspired by their forthcoming musical *Jeeves*. And couturier Hardy Amies, whose salon was on Savile Row's sunny side, crossed the road to have a suit made. Nutter's other clients included a number of titled men-about-town as well as London's Peacocks.

Nutter displayed a little boy quality that seemed innocently straightforward. If he was shrewd in business, it did not show socially. The shop's clothes were priced in line with their neighbours: a suit from £140, dinner jacket and trousers from £200. Such prices were considered expensive at the time, but due to high overheads, so Nutter claimed, profit margins were modest. A shirt shop, developed competitively along the lines of Mr Fish, proved a costly mistake and was closed quickly without fuss.

As the 1970s began the bespoke business remained steady. Plans were in hand to branch out into ready-to-wear, the clothes to be marketed through Austin Reed's flagship store on Regent Street, when in 1974 there was a coup behind closed doors. Tommy Nutter was out. His surname would survive in golden letters across the shop window for some years to come, but he was no longer there. Kilgour, French & Stanbury, across the road, took him in.

Nutter died in August 1992 and Sexton re-established himself elsewhere as a tailor of note using his own name. Until the arrival of Richard James in the 1990s (with backing from Sir Elton John), the pair at Nutters had formed one of the most creative tailoring teams in the Row's recent history.

Opposite Red velvet jacket with red ribbon edging and jewelled buttons. With waistcoat. £110. To order at Nutters, Savile Row, W1. Shirt from a range at David Elliott, Shepherd Street. Embroidered trousers in red, yellow and white. £26 5s at Dean Rogers, 6 Thayer Street. Photograph: Peter Rand.

CHAPTER 4
And Then It Ended

1970–75

With the dawn of the 1970s the Peacock Revolution began to lose momentum. The concept that fashionable clothes for men could exist in a world parallel to that of women's fashion had turned into reality, and the inner circle that had come visually to epitomize London's fashion-minded originals simply dropped out of the limelight, becoming well-dressed men with unassuming public profiles. Some disappeared into middle-class Britain accepting the commitments of work and the responsibilities of young families just as their fathers had. London was no longer the Swinging place it had been.

A new breed of commercial players had commandeered the marketplace, turning their attention away from the recent years of liberated fancy dress that had encompassed Mods, Teds, Peacocks and Flower Power children as well as Glam Rock fans, aping the image of their adored pop stars. Even the Skinheads, who had taken to the King's Road and made their punk presence felt with the encouragement of Malcolm McLaren and Vivienne Westwood (their shop had once been the premises of the exotic Peacock sanctum, Hung on You), were in decline.

By the very nature of their intensely fashionable premises, the days of idiosyncratic boutiques were numbered. The end was nigh. Fashion comes and fashion goes; it was ever thus. Some of the Peacocks' favourite clothes could still be found, but their suppliers were fast disappearing. Replacing them were shops selling designer-label merchandise from Europe. Soon there would be an invasion from the United States. Men's fashion had gone legitimate and named designers were creating heavily-promoted, attainable images that were photographed by the world's leading photographers and reproduced in magazines that were devoting countless pages to fashion. Nino Cerruti and Yves Saint Laurent had heralded the arrival of international brands and franchises but they, too, in a few years would be superceded by a new wave of professionals with solid, organizational support. Young blood with a clear image of how men should dress, such as Giorgio Armani and Ralph Lauren, hovered, ready to assume the mantle of international designer fame. Smart clothes replaced flamboyance.

The Swinging Sixties had encouraged opportunistic amateurs to play and have fun, and for some men, from Mod to Peacock, this made fashion awareness an integral part of their lives. The mid-1970s, however, introduced the first intimations of a move to materialism as an overweening desire to make money became apparent. With divisions elbowed aside, everyone blended – in theory, if not practice. Manufacturers generally became more adventurous, and retailers began to replace eccentric boutiques with shops where both buyers and management could see that fashion was simply business. While Chelsea had gentrified and real estate prices reflected the borough's worth, the King's Road was no longer a place of parade. It had turned itself into another

Opposite Pink cotton cowboy shirt, £4, blue and white checked cotton trousers, £6. All by John Weitz, at Austin Reed, Regent St. *Men in Vogue*, 15 March 1966. Photograph: Ron Traeger.

high street, with clothes shops like any other. In a weary moment in January 1975, as his Clifford Street shop was closing down with a sale, Michael Fish summed up the transience of the Peacock moment: 'Fashion,' he said, 'doesn't exist any more. Only clothes'.

As Tom Gilbey would later say about the players who had attempted to harness the Peacock world in the 1960s and make it a lasting period of history: 'The energy was there, not the talent. Or the understanding of commerce. It was energy that was driving everyone, nothing else'.

For survivors, looking back, it was not all gloom. With smiles, and fond if fading memories, they remember what can only be considered the Good Times. As an era, the period from 1963 to 1973 never seemed as important then as it does now. Few designers kept examples of their work, few kept photographs of even the newspaper cuttings that might have been proof of their extended moments of fame. Kenneth Williams, who would become managing director of Turnbull & Asser in Jermyn Street, ruefully but bluntly puts the period into context, summing up the short life of the Peacock world of fashion, fun and flamboyance: 'Business,' he says, 'wasn't serious in those days'.

Perhaps the last words should go to Mary Hopkin, who sang at the end of the decade: 'Those were the days my friend, we thought they'd never end,' but end they did. Amateurs some may have been, sensing a new spirit in fashion and plunging in. Others formed a new breed of entrepreneurs, combining traditional tailoring with the design flair of fashion graduates. All were driven by an energy and enthusiasm. And the result was a new style of dress for a modern dandy, whose flamboyant wardrobe mirrored the creative atmosphere of the time.

Above Fur-lined black canvas coat over denim jacket with quilted trim and modified jodhpurs. From Yves Saint Laurent collection, 1972. Private collection.

Above Ken Swift in a slim suit for a Hardy Amies fashion show. Hardy Amies Archive.

Above Edward Fox, actor, wears double-breasted cashmere cardigan with covered buttons, £27 6s, with check trousers, 8gns. At John Michael. *Men in Vogue*, November 1965. Photograph: Norman Parkinson/Parkinson Archive.

Above For the Hepworth collection in 1968, Hardy Amies teamed high buttoning tweed jackets with casual trousers, often in bold checks. Hardy Amies Archive.

Opposite Corin Redgrave, actor, in Jaeger's Hebridean herringbone tweed suit. Jacket 18gns, cigarette-shaped trousers, 9gns. *Men in Vogue*, November 1965. Photograph: Norman Parkinson/ Parkinson Archive.

Above Jay Johnson in blazer with white-braiding, £11, and white baggies, £10, by Gordon Deighton for Harrods. Polka-dot shirt and contrasting tie from Turnbull & Asser. *Evening Standard*, 24 March 1972. Photograph: Roy Jones/*Evening Standard*/Getty Images.

Opposite Dark, lean and handsome formality. Smoothly double-breasted grey chalk-stripe worsted suit. Narrow shouldered jacket with wide lapels; high rise trousers cut straight and narrow. From Cue at Austin Reed. Shirt in grey silk crepe striped finely with red and white, worn with matching tie, Turnbull & Asser. *Vogue*, 15 September 1967. Photograph: David Montgomery.

Index

References followed by a *c* refer to captions.

Photographic credits

All images are © V&A Images unless noted otherwise

© Hardy Amies archive: pp.28, 136 (right), 138; © Celia Birtwell collection: p.18; © Michael Cooper / Vogue © The Condé Nast Publications Ltd: pp.50, 54; © Photograph Colin Davey, Camera Press London: p.41; © Barry Fantoni: p.6; © Fashion Museum, Bath: pp.35 (left), 40, 44, 49, 65, 77 (left), 94, 95, 100, 111, 116;

Photograph: Hans Feurer: 124; © Getty Images: pp.29, 30, 31, 32, 37, 47, 51, 71, 73, 77 (right), 83 (left), 90, 92, 93, 103, 123, 128, 130, 131, 140; © Denis Gooden / Vogue © The Condé Nast Publications Ltd: p.2; © Patrick Litchfield / Vogue © The Condé Nast Publications Ltd: pp.62, 114; © MirrorPix: p.72; © David

Montgomery / Vogue © The Condé Nast Publications Ltd: p.140; © Courtesy of Norman Parkinson Archive: pp.134, 139; Private collection: pp.24 (right), 25, 38, 39, 48, 66, 67, 79 (left), 83 (right), 84, 104, 109, 112, 113, 120, 121, 136 (left); Private collection. Photograph Manolo Blahnik: p.79 (right); Private collection.

Photograph Roy Jones: p.118; © Photograph Peter Rand: pp.33 (right), 35 (right), 52, 53, 56, 57, 58, 59, 60, 61, 98, 99, 106, 124, 132; © Rex Features: pp.33 (left), 45, 55, 86, 115; © Topfoto: p.89; © Photograph Ron Traeger: pp.14, 23, 63, 68, 70, 74, 76, 78, 134; © Turnbull and Asser Archive: pp.20, 21, 96, 107